Demystifying the Cue

Thoughts and strategies for creating competitive
Film and TV music in today's new media world

Dean Krippaehne

Copyright © 2014 Dean Krippaehne

All rights reserved. No part of this book may be reproduced in any form, without written permission, except by a newspaper, magazine or digital media reviewer who wishes to quote a brief passage in connection with a review.

Published by RMC Publishing
21040 Fifth Avenue South
Seattle, Washington 98198 USA
www.retromediacollective.com

Library of Congress cataloging data available upon request.

ISBN: 1500686107
ISBN-13: 978-1500686109

CONTENTS

INTRODUCTION

1	Demystifying the Music Cue	3
2	The Main Thing	7

PRODUCTION CONCEPTS

3	Raising the Bar – Quality or Quickly	10
4	Don't Funk with the Feel	14
5	The Importance of Well Defined Moods	18

RECORDING TIPS AND TRICKS

6	A Few Good Tricks	24
7	Pulling My Hair Out	27
8	Virtual Instruments and Golf Clubs	31
9	Blackberry Cobbler - Templates	36
10	Accentuate the Positive (Recording the Vocalist)	42
11	How I Record My Guitar	49
12	Mixing the Bass	58
13	Pushing Air - Big Sound	64
14	Panning	67
15	The Arrangement (Don't Forget About It)	71
16	Turning a Demo Into a Master	74
17	Cataloging Music Samples (Saving Time)	79
18	Anatomy of a Redneck Track	83
19	Collaboration	87
20	Imperfections	90

ON SECOND LISTEN

21	CaffeeVanillaCaramelMochaMacchiatoCon...	94
22	Clutter	98
23	Spoons	103
24	Fido Nashville (Less is More Unless More is More)	106

FURTHERMORE
25	Ricky & Lucy and The Ten Foot Bow	110

SONGWRITERS TIPS & TRICKS
26	Light Bulbs - Film and TV Songwriting Lyrics	116
27	Songs for Sinatra	121
28	If a Picture Paints a Thousand Words (Visualizing)	126
29	Step Away from the Song (Song REwriting)	132
30	Free Falling - When One Small Thing Can Be BIG	135
31	Somethin' 'Bout a Truck (Breaking Rules)	138
32	Meh! I Have Nothing to Say (Songwriting Frustration)	141

THE CREATIVE PROCESS
33	Top 5 Personality Traits in Songwriting	146
34	Writer's Roadblock	148
35	Dropping Needles	150
36	Failing Quickly	153
37	Connecting the Dots	156
38	12 Notes	160

THE BIZ
39	Stuff Changes	165
40	Digital Fingerprinting	169
41	Risky Business	174
42	The Ten Commandments and the Music Biz	177
43	Lost in Translation	183
44	Diversify	187
45	More on Diversification in the Music Business	193
46	The Perception of Quality	197
47	Greatest Hits? (In a Music Library)	203
48	Networking	207
49	Music Royalties (The Good, the Bad and the Ugly)	213

CULTURAL CHANGES, SHIFTING SANDS
50	Where Did the Cheese Go?	220
51	Get Your Brand New Space Age iPhone Transistor Radio	227
52	Here There and Everywhere	232

PSYCHOLOGY, SOCIOLOGY AND PERSPECTIVE

53	Do These Songs Make My Music Look Phat?	237
54	Rejection (Learning to Deal with Disappointment)	242
55	Isn't This Supposed to Be Fun?	248
56	Can One Small Change Make a Big Difference?	252
57	A New Perspective	255
58	Making Molehills out of Mountains	261
59	Making a List – Checking it Twice	264
60	Inspiration or Perspiration?	268
61	Moods	272
62	Resources	276
63	Conclusion	278
	Acknowledgments	279
	Glossary	280
	Bibliography	282

Demystifying the Cue

INTRODUCTION

It's been over a decade since I placed my first song in the daytime soap *One Life To Live* (ABC). At that time I had absolutely no idea what the TV music business was all about or that there was some weird thing called a "cue" used in TV shows. Up until then I was like many in my field: I was a songwriter trying to get cuts and an indie artist trying to get heard.

My eyes began to open when I received my first royalty check for *One Life to Live*. I noticed that one particular song of mine had been used three times in a single episode. I also noticed that *each* of those three usages paid *its own separate royalty*.

What?! I can get paid three separate times on the same song just because it is being used in different places on the same show? There must be some mistake.

Thus began my journey into the world of Film and TV music.

I have since placed thousands of cues and songs in TV shows and other media and have gathered a bag full of tricks, tips and useful knowledge about what it takes to make this happen.

Hence, this book.

I have been lucky enough to get to know many generous people in the music biz who have helped me tremendously along my path. They have picked me up when I have fallen and taught me both the rules of the road and tricks of the trade. It now seems like it is my turn to pass along these insights I have learned.

This book is filled with the kinds of things that can help you take years off your road to "getting there." It is my hope that the information in these pages will help you avoid some potholes and pitfalls along the way and possibly pave a smoother highway toward your musical destination.

I should tell you a bit about this book - what it is, and what it is not. This is not a book that talks about specific EQ and compression settings. It does not suggest the best reverbs to use nor the depth and length to set them. There are plenty of great recording engineer books out there that will tell you those kinds of things.

This book is for the artist who is already doing some of that but has either become stuck or simply wants to learn some tips and tricks to getting better – and faster. It is also for the producer who wants to get bigger sounding tracks, the songwriter who wants to hone their skills for Film and TV placements, the singer who needs a little push in business of networking and the creative whose weakness is in organization and work habits. In addition these chapters are for any creative person who wants to better understand what music to work on and what music to let go of and for anyone else who wants to discern what they are spending too much time on and what deserves a little more of their attention.

If this is you – if you want to move ahead more quickly than you have been – then you are in the right place.

One more thing I should tell you about this book. The chapters are not written in any particular chronological order. That means you can basically start reading anywhere. Pick one chapter of interest and begin there. You will be just fine. I am kind of an ADD thinker and some my chapters follow my illogical thought path.

That's about it. Welcome aboard. Let's learn something together, get better, make some great music and grow our bank accounts.

Dean Krippaehne

Demystifying the Music Cue

What is a music cue?

I get asked this question a lot.

Honestly, it took me many years to figure out exactly what a music cue was in terms of modern day TV programming. And it took me a while longer to figure out what a music cue *wasn't*.

There is often confusion about what exactly a TV music cue is. Perhaps this is because a cue is often called many different things. Sometimes it is called a "track" or a "song." I've heard people refer to a cue as a "composition," a "needle drop," an "instrumental," and even just plain "crappy."

None of these titles are necessarily incorrect. In fact, I will use many of them interchangeably throughout this book. But for the sake of this introduction's definition I will simply call any slice of music used in a modern day TV show a *cue*. (As in, "Cue the music please!")

I am going to try to lay out some general things I have learned about TV music cues but before I do I must preface my comments by stating that there are no hard and fast absolutes here as to what a good cue is or isn't.

My number one rule for writing and producing any kind of music is *If it works, it works - and if it doesn't, well...*

Let's start out by examining what a cue most likely is *not*.

Songs

The majority of music cues used in TV are not what a songwriter or a recording artist would typically refer to as a *song*, although some cues are in fact songs. A typical Pop song has a couple verses and a chorus with possibly a bridge section. It also usually has a vocalist singing or rapping lyrics.

A typical music cue will have only one mood section and no lyrics. (Note that *vocal songs* are indeed used as cues in TV shows but instrumentals outnumber them by *at least* a 10 to 1 ratio.)

There are a couple good reasons why instrumental music cues far outnumber vocal music cues. First of all, songs with vocals and lyrics can often get in the way of an actor's dialogue. Music supervisors need to be very careful where and how they use vocal songs so they don't compete for attention with an actor's dialogue, thereby ruining a scene.

Secondly, most TV show scenes want to highlight one particular mood or emotion at a time. Often when a Pop song moves from verse to chorus its mood and emotion will change.

So in the loosest sense of the word a cue may indeed be a song - but it is not often like your typical pop song.

Compositions

Traditionally speaking, composers in the film business were thought of as the ones who wrote the score, or all of the music for an entire film. John Williams (*Star Wars, Raiders of the Lost Ark*) and Bill Conti (*Rocky, Dynasty*) are the guys who come to my mind when thinking of typical film and TV composers.

While writing an instrumental cue may indeed be defined as

composing it is usually not referred to as a *composition* in the traditional sense of the word. A cue used in a TV show tends to be *at the most* only about two minutes in length. So it is, at least in this way, quite dissimilar to the stereotypical definition of a film composer's score.

In addition, most movies have peaks and valleys in their instrumental movements whereas the majority of cues maintain the same mood throughout the entire composition.

Granted, many cues sound like traditional movie scores - especially the dramatic, action packed movie trailer music cues with their booming percussion and soaring orchestras. I have heard many cue compositions of this type that would rival the best movie scores in both their creative value as well as their sonic professionalism.

Cues

What then is a cue?

A music cue (as produced by an artist or music library) is most commonly defined in today's TV market as a piece of music about two minutes in length that highlights one particular mood or a combination of similar moods. (Such as a tense/action/chase/fear music cue, or a sad/melancholy/loss music cue.)

A typical cue also ends with a "stinger." That means it does not fade out. Many TV show music editors like to punctuate a scene with a "sting" or a full band-chord that hits quick with little to no sustain. Usually this chord is the root of whatever key the cue is written in. (I.e. if the cue is played in the key of C major then the stinger chord will also be a C major chord). If the music editor wants the music to fade he or she can fade the cue wherever they desire.

Sometimes an entire two minute cue is used in a TV show's scene but more often than not only a 20, 30, or 40 second slice is used.

A cue may or may not have vocals in it. Some cues will maintain movement without building or lifting the mood but quite often a cue will build every four to eight measures to intensify whatever emotion it is conveying.

This can be done through melody, rhythmic elements and instrumental dynamics or by adding and subtracting musical instruments. There are dozens of additional production techniques used to help accomplish this type of mood intensification many of which we will address later.

Parameters

Let me reiterate that any parameters or rules I may communicate to you about what a cue is or isn't can and will be broken. If the cue is cool and a music supervisor likes it and uses it in a TV show - then it is right. And if it elevates the scene without drawing attention to itself – it is *great!*

It should be noted, too, that cues can be used as both background music in a scene or as foreground music.

Got it?

Let's move on.

The Main Thing

In the editor's blog of *Recording Magazine* an enticing question was recently posed:

What really makes a great recording?

The magazine's blog proposed that if you were to give a truly great recording artist (à la Paul McCartney, Joni Mitchell or Stevie Wonder) a cassette tape recorder and ask them to go into a room and record something they would come out an hour later or so with a very cool sounding recording. Maybe not an award winner – but a great recording nevertheless.

Their point was this: it doesn't take a lot of bells and whistles to make a great recording, it takes *talent*.

In other words what makes a great recording is YOU.

Gear Geeks

I think what *Recording Magazine*'s blog author was getting at is that we songwriters, composers, producers and artists now have – with the advent of digital recording technology – world class studios in our own homes and at our fingertips. As a consequence many of us have become "gear geeks."

We have become infatuated with our new software, our Pro Tools and Kontakt, our flashy plugins and fancy mastering processors. It has become fairly common when one of our productions doesn't sound quite right to start looking for a *digital* solution.

"Maybe if I use a different kick or snare it will give the song more punch," we say to ourselves.

"I think I need to get East West Strings. Surely then my compositions will sound more real and more alive."

Sometimes a digital solution is the correct answer but more often than not it is not the best way to address our recording problems.

It's Not the Gear, it's the Ear

I think *Recording Magazine*'s blog author knows that when we talk about *just needing some better software* we are often fooling ourselves. We are taking our eyes off the ball and blowing our chance to get better at our craft.

I think, too, what he is getting at is *it is not the gear that makes something great*. What makes a recording great is a well written song, the perfect arrangement, a stellar performance and a killer vibe. Those are the things that will make our music jump out of the speakers and dance.

I don't think the author is implying that it is only Paul McCartney, Stevie Wonder and the rest of the music legends who create great music. I would have to disagree with him if that was his point. Instead, what the author is suggesting to us is that these music masters "got it right."

They wrote great songs, played their instruments with passion and sang their lyrics with a soulful delivery before they ever stepped into a studio. The studio for them was simply a way to capture greatness and document it for others to appreciate.

The Main Thing

It is easy for us to lose sight of this truth. Mozart, Beethoven, Frank Sinatra and the Beatles did not have digital recording studios and sweet sounding software in their heydays. What they had was the perseverance to develop their talents, their songs and their performances to the highest levels - and then, and only then - put the final ink to paper or music to tape.

We now have in our homes and at our fingertips studio gear equivalent to what used to cost millions of dollars. But let us not forget the main thing. Let's remember to always keep in mind the things that will truly touch the hearts and minds of our audience. Things like a great song (or cue), a perfect arrangement and a passionate performance.

May we as artists and technicians always be vigilant in our remembrance of this: The main thing is to keep the main thing the main thing.

Raising the Bar - Quality or Quickly

Have you ever listened to the way people discuss Steve Jobs - especially those who have worked with him?

Not a lot of people talk about how much they *liked* Steve Jobs as a person and yet he is widely respected and admired throughout the entire world.

Why?

He is and was admired at least in part because he built GREAT stuff for you and for me to use. And because he built us this great stuff we perceive him as *caring* about us and our needs.

I love the phrase "people don't care what you know until they know that you care."
I think this phrase is a true life statement as well as a pretty good business mission statement.

If we can somehow show the people in our lives (or our customers and clients) that we care about them and their needs they will then quite possibly be interested in examining whatever it is we have to offer.

Fast Tracks

We as producers of music are all trying to *sell* our productions somewhere. Some of us are trying to sell a few tracks to the Film and TV folks and others are trying to get a song placed with a recording artist or two.

Since many of the people to whom we are selling our wares don't know us at all, how then are we to let them know we care?

We let them know we care by creating *quality* music. When we create music that is well written, well recorded, well produced, well mixed and well mastered we send them a loud and clear message - *we care*. We let them know immediately through our well crafted music that we value our product and have great confidence in its ability to help them achieve their goals.

A lot of my advice in music production is aimed at helping you to get *faster* at what you do. The reason for this, generally speaking, is that you need to produce a lot of cues to make a decent amount of money. In addition, there are times when you will be faced with deadlines where you only have a matter of hours to write, produce and deliver your music to a client.

However, even though I will often focus on the ways in which we can become faster at producing our music, it cannot be overstated that *speed should never come at the expense of quality*.

Raising the Bar

Let me ask you a few questions. What, if anything, is there about the production you are currently working on that can be made better? Could the performance level of one of the instruments be raised up a few notches? Maybe the guitar part isn't quite tight enough. Are you going to shoot for a better guitar part or leave it as is?

Maybe it's something in the mix. Is there too much reverb on one or more or your sounds? Is the song drowning in wetness and becoming smaller sounding instead of bigger sounding? Or maybe it is too dry. Maybe you were going for that *up close and intimate feel* but the lead vocal is just a little too dry and you need a little bit more depth to it. Are you going to remix it and get the vocal perfect or leave it as is and be done with it?

Here's a hint – redo it! Raise the bar. Make it better. Make it the best it can be.

Maybe it's a song you are writing. Is your lyric perfect? Can it be better? When you are listening to the melody are you thinking, "ok, that works" or are you smiling and exclaiming, "wow – that is killer!?"

Maybe your lyric says "*I hope you will always love me.*" What you happen to the meaning of your song if you tried changing it to "*I had hoped you would always love me.*" Have you tried every lyric option to find something magical or have you simply settled for what works?

Make it better - or at least try to make it better.

In addition to taking this quality approach in writing and recording we should also strive for quality in our business relationships. We will benefit greatly if we always make certain that we are representing ourselves as quality professionals in every aspect of our careers. Most people we work with will recognize and appreciate this and will want to work with us again and again.

Too Perfectionist

Of course, having said all of that, it should also be stated that we need to be aware of the possibility of being too perfectionist. In its extreme, perfectionism can lead to procrastination which in turn can lead to paralysis. In other words, if we let our perfectionism take us over we will never get anything done because of the simple fact that nothing we ever produce will be absolutely perfect.

The best we can do is to keep raising the bar on ourselves and get our creations to be the absolute best they can possibly be. Once we have done this we need to then let them go and move on.

Don't Funk With The Feel

Have you ever gone to church?

Yes? No?

Have you ever gone to any event where a pretty good speaker is doing their thing?
Can you feel yourself sitting there listening to that speaker or preacher draw you into the story - deep into a mood or an emotion - where you are so entranced you're unaware of yourself and your surroundings? Do you recall how you felt when suddenly their microphone cuts out or the PA screeches an annoying feedback sound?

What happens to you at this precise moment?

If you are like me all of your thoughts are immediately snapped out of their contemplative flow, cut off from their beautiful bliss and the only thing you are thinking about is how stupid and irritating the PA system is.

Romance

Another question.

Have you ever been moving down some romantic evening's

passionate path with your loved one - soft lights glowing, sultry music simmering, a couple of glasses of excellent wine - you know the scene - when suddenly that beautiful, perfect person whose eyes you are gazing into questions the thirteen hundred bucks you want to spend on "yet another silly guitar?"

Have you ever then listened to them as they go on to explain how this $1,300 would be much better spent on purchasing some used couch they have just discovered on Craigslist? (Not that this has ever happened to me...)

What happens next?

Feelings start to simmer, battle lines are drawn, old irritations get reignited and walls go up.

It can be a mood killer.

Situational *flow* can come to a grinding halt in a second. It doesn't take much to alter a mood.

Background Music for TV

One of the main things I often hear new composers and producers doing wrong in their otherwise good productions is drastically shifting the mood or tempo in their songs.

I have heard some truly great productions grooving pleasantly along in a 4/4 teen-pop-rock feel when suddenly without warning the track abruptly shift gears and turns into some kind of weird Carribean bossa-nova feel. This dramatic change-up is so shocking to my sensibilities I have actually had the physical reaction of ripping off my headphones in utter befuddlement.

The best advice I can give to songwriters and producers who indulge in this kind of artistic license when creating background music for Film and TV is: "Stop it."

Unless you have been hired to score and orchestrate an entire movie and are working side by side with the film's director – don't alter the vibe or the time signature. Don't mess with the groove. Don't funk with the feel.

Music Supervisors

When a music supervisor hears a piece of music he or she needs to know immediately what the mood is. It needs to be utterly obvious. That mood then needs to sustain or build throughout the entire track.

If a music supervisor needs to change the mood in a scene they will simply grab an additional piece of music with the different desired mood and insert it precisely at the point in the scene where they want the emotional change.

Trust me on this. Changing moods or the vibe or the feel of your track will do nothing except make you look like an amateur to the very people you want to look professional to.

Bee Gees

"But Dean, it is so cool to have my song change moods. Lots of hits from big time artists have done this – why can't I?"

Yes, many hit songs throughout the history of radio have changed tempos and feels. (See: Bee Gees' "Nights on Broadway," Godspell's "Day by Day," Adele's "Rumor Has It," or the Doobies' "Jesus is Just Alright" ...the list goes on and on). These songs with their mood changes are cool for what they are, which is *radio* hits. But they do not work well as background mood tracks in current Film and TV shows.

If a music supervisor and director desires those exact mood changes they will probably just license a particular hit song from the original artist. And that specific hit song will often be used as *foreground* music as opposed to being a background mood enhancer.

Stick with the mood.

Whatever emotion you are trying to convey in your song – stay there. Build that vibe and feel, give it motion and interest, but stick with the mood you started with.

You don't want to be the guy who says (just as his dream date is about to lay her first kiss on him) "Hey, how about that grand slam in the Sox game last night?"

Buzz kill.

Stick with the mood.

Go with the flow.

Don't rock the boat or rattle the cage.

...at least not in your Film and TV cues.

The Importance of Well Defined Moods

Are you depressed?

Anxious?

Tense?

Melancholy?

Happy and excited?

Over the years I have noticed a trend with my instrumental music cues. The more strongly defined they are to fit a particular emotion the more frequently they are used.

Spreadsheets

Most of us who have been producing music for production libraries are quite familiar with spreadsheets.

For those of you who have not yet had the pleasure (cough, cough) of filling out a spreadsheet for a music library let me give you a brief description of the process: it is hell! Well, not really. It used to feel like hell when we actually had to fill out real spreadsheets and type in all of the information for each individual cue but most libraries have now turned their spreadsheets into simple drop-down menu forms online which are quite easy to use.

With these drop-down menus a cue's information can now be filled out in just a minute or two.

Accurate information for each cue you've produced is needed so that a music supervisor (the person who picks the music for a film or TV show) can easily and quickly find the exact type of music he or she is looking for. It is also needed so that your cue can be reported properly to a PRO (Performing Rights Organization) and they can in turn cut you a check.

The kinds of information needed for each track are things like beats per minute (bpm), musical key, genre, publishing information, songwriter info, PRO affiliation (ASCAP, BMI, etc.), lead instruments, is it vocal or instrumental, and the mood and description of the song.

I should also note here that music libraries and supervisors will all have their own file format(s) in which they wish to receive your music. (As well as sampling and bit rate preferences.) Some will request WAV or MP3 and others will request AIFF or some other file format. Always find out the specifics from anyone you are working with and export your music accordingly. Most all of the modern day DAWs allow you to export your music to any one of the commonly used file formats.

Having said that, it is the mood or *emotion* of a song that I want to talk a bit about now.

Iffy

When I first started writing and recording cues for TV I didn't think too much about the mood I was creating. I was just trying to make my music sound good. Because of this approach I soon found that every once in a while one of my songs really didn't fit any one particular emotion or mood at all. The song may have sounded pleasant enough but it really didn't jump out and say,

"I'm scary," or "I'm tense and apprehensive," or "I'm going to be mischievous in a comical way."

I was stuck in mood no-man's land.

These songs were quite troubling to try to categorize. I recall thinking to myself, "well, this song is kind of tense, but not *really* tense and it might make someone feel a little bit of apprehension but only *a little*." I would, of course, need to choose moods for these songs when I was filling out spreadsheets but picking exactly the correct moods always left me feeling like I had somehow missed the mark.

These songs fell in between the cracks, so to speak, and as I would later find out they usually did *miss the mark*. They did not get placed in any TV shows.

When you think about it, if you were a music supervisor who needed a piece of music for a *tense* scene where the characters are full of apprehension, would you pick a cue that was maybe, kinda tense and a little apprehensive or would you pick one that hit the tense and apprehensive mark dead on? You'd pick the dead on cue – every time.

Nailing It

On the other hand, when I have recorded a cue that absolutely nails a mood it stands a really good chance of getting placed in a show – multiple times.

How do I know if it hits the mark? I usually know when I am filling out the moods section of a drop-down menu spreadsheet and my song seems to fit *perfectly* for multiple similar descriptors.

For example, if I have written a tension track and it not only fits perfectly for "tension" but also fits quite well for other related emotions like apprehensive, suspenseful, anxious, fearful and danger – I am probably on the money.

If I say to you I have written a dramedy piece that sounds quirky, playful, sneaky, light and comedic – you can most likely already hear the music in your mind without ever hearing my track.

Accuracy

When submitting cues to music libraries or music supervisors we must take great care in trying to be as accurate with our mood identifiers as possible. If we have labeled a cue as funny, mischievous and quirky when it is actually quite tense and apprehensive just because we think that someone could use it in a dark comedy – we may be shooting ourselves in the proverbial foot.

If a music supervisor listens to that track because they are looking for something quirky and mischievous and they hear something tense and apprehensive they may think, "WTF!?!"

We will have wasted their time and run the risk of alienating ourselves and our production library from them.

Be accurate when describing your cues.

Helpful Tips

When I am going into the studio to produce a tension track (for example) it is helpful for me to take along a list of tension moods and read them over and over again as I am writing and recording. The list might look like this:

Tense
Fearful
Aggressive
Suspenseful
Anxious
Apprehensive
Danger
Dark
Chase

That list will help me to more clearly imagine what those moods might sound like so I can more sharply define my track's mood as I go.

My list when I go in to record a dramedy cue might look like this:

Sneaky
Quirky
Playful
Funny
Fun
Mischief
Comedic

As I am recording, the music may start to lean more strongly towards two or three of those words. That is okay. In fact, that is good. What we are trying to do is articulate a specific emotion that the characters in a TV scene are feeling in the best musical way possible. The more accurately we can pinpoint a couple of those mood keywords the better chance our music has of being used.

Donkey

When you finally pin the tail on the donkey of any given mood for your music the rewards can be cool indeed. I have some pieces that have been used in TV shows dozens and dozens of times.

Go out there and get it.

Hit your mood's mark!

Pin the tail on that donkey.

Takeaways (Chapters 1 – 5)

1. A cue can be a song or a composition.

2. A typical cue is most often about two minutes in length.

3. A typical cue ends with a stinger on the dominant or root chord.

4. You are what makes great music – not your gear.

5. Always strive for the quality over quantity in all areas of music production.

6. Keep a cue's mood and vibe consistent throughout.

7. Don't alter the time signature or tempo of a cue.

8. Try to accurately convey one particular mood (or closely related moods) in a cue.

9. Accurately label your cue's mood when filling out spreadsheets.

10. Accurately fill out all of your cue's information when submitting to music library or supervisor.

11. Mix and send your music in the file format requested by your client.

A Few Good Tricks

I love great acting.

I love great movies.

Did you ever see the movie *A Few Good Men*?

Do you remember the final dramatic courtroom scene?

The one where Tom Cruise and Jack Nicholson's characters are arguing...

I love it when Tom Cruise's character says, "I want the truth!"

And Jack Nicholson's character screams back at him, "You can't handle the truth!"

Wow!

That is believable stuff!

If you have seen this movie you know the realism and intensity of that particular moment.

The emotional exchange is frighteningly palpable and so *very* believable. Yet it wasn't real. It was simply two highly skilled actors at the top of their game with a wonderful script, great direction, perfect courtroom setting, excellent lighting, brilliant wardrobe and flawless camera angles all working together to *trick* us into believing this scene - this story - was real.

Virtual Instruments

A big part of our job when we are recording with virtual instruments instead of using *real* players and real instruments is to make our virtual instruments sound absolutely believable. There are many things we must articulate with each instrument to accomplish this but one often overlooked practice involves what I call *tricking* the listener's ear into believing that all of your virtual instruments are real.

This music production technique is quite simple. All you have to do is add at least one *real* instrument to the track or song you are working on - preferably in the intro - and all of your virtual instruments will magically sound much more realistic.

Your latest, greatest virtual instruments may indeed sound awesome all by themselves but they are still just samples. Even if they are well articulated, adding a *real instrument* to the mix will trick the listener's ear into thinking all of the instruments must be real. It will make your samples and your song sound even better.

Guitars

I have been amazed by the high quality of some of today's guitar samples. It would take me hours and hours of experimentation with tones, pickups, amplifiers, microphone techniques and mic combinations to come close to the way some of these wonderfully sampled virtual guitars sound. I will use them quite often.

But even if I play these guitar samples (on the keyboard) exactly as a guitar player would play and articulate them, they still sound slightly "stiff."

However, if I add a *real* guitar at the beginning of the song (to trick the listener's ear), all of my sampled guitars somehow sound magically better - like real players. I am not sure of the physics or biology behind this phenomenon but it works every time.

Also, if you are using a truly great string library and have articulated your strings to utter perfection you can make those strings sound even *more* believable by adding a *real* viola or violin player to the mix. Doubling one of the virtual parts with a live player will breathe a reality into your track that is incredible and undeniable.

Lately I have been recording a lot of horn section tracks. For my virtual instruments I have been using a combination of Sample-Modeling Horns and Mojo Horn Section for both my swing and funk tracks. It is amazing what hiring one sax player will do to make those tracks truly *pop* or *jump* in a completely believable way. A sax player or a trumpet player actually blowing air through his or her horn and into a microphone with all of their wonderful human nuances and imperfections mixed with your virtual horn section will do the trick time and time again.

Sure, I would like to hire a real horn section - that would be optimal - but quite often the projects I am working on do not have the budget it would take to hire a horn section so it is not usually an option.

Try It Out

If you have not yet implemented this trick into your recordings I suggest you give it a try. Even a one note, one finger, real guitar part mixed in with your samples will make your virtual instruments sound better.

That is the truth.

I know you can handle the truth.

Pulling My Hair Out

While hanging out with some recording engineer friends at the NAB conference in Las Vegas recently the subject came up about whether it was better to convert your MIDI tracks (Musical Instrument Digital Interface – aka: Virtual Instruments) to audio tracks, or just leave them as is.

Although there were many opinions and arguments brought forth pertaining to quality issues (i.e. which sounds better - mixing directly from midi virtual instruments or converting midi to audio files and then mixing), there was one important argument *in favor* of converting midi to audio I found to be the most compelling.

It was something all of us who have been recording digitally for the last decade or so have had to deal with and a lesson that many of us, including myself, have had to learn the hard way. I'll give you the condensed version example of what I am referring to.

Ouch

Back in 2003 I had recorded what I thought were some pretty cool sounding songs for a CCM project. I, however, did not convert any of the midi tracks in those songs to audio. I left the drums, bass, keys, strings, pads, etc... in their virgin midi state. The only tracks on these songs that were recorded in audio were the guitars and vocals.

A couple of years ago I had an opportunity to place one of these old songs on a TV show. The only hitch for this particular placement was that I would need to remix the song and provide a new mix of the song without vocals.

No problem, right?

Wrong.

When I brought up the old song file and its individual tracks in my DAW (Digital Audio Workstation), not only was I bringing up a *way* outdated version of my DAW which didn't line up very well with my new upgraded version, but most of the midi tracks were recorded with virtual instrument software I no longer even owned. I had long since replaced this software with newer software and better sounding virtual instrument samples. In addition, I was running everything on an entirely new computer operating system. Yikes.
I was in a bind.

Although all of the midi information was intact and I could cue up new virtual instruments if I wanted to, it would take a monumental amount of reconfiguring to get these new tracks and instruments to sound like the old ones. This was a problem because it was the old song's sounds the music supervisor had fallen in love with.

If, however, back in 2003 I would have converted all of my midi tracks to audio tracks, remixing the song would have been a snap. I could have simply brought up the audio tracks in my DAW and started mixing.

Lesson Learned

Converting midi to audio these days is incredibly easy. Just refer to your DAW's manual and you will find it is a very simple process.

I don't want you to think I am saying this process *needs* to be done - it does not. I am only giving you one example of a potential derailment - if you will - that you may experience should you need to recall an old mix years after you have upgraded systems, uninstalled old software and installed brand new stuff.

An additional benefit of converting midi tracks to audio tracks is that in these days of cross country and around the world collaborations with multiple producers using different DAWs, exchanging audio files through the internet opens up a variety of opportunities. Audio files are pretty universal. They will work in almost anyone's recording system.

Certainly midi information, because of its small size, is quite easy to send through the web but unless your collaborator has the identical virtual instrument software as you, it will just be a transfer of *information* - not *sounds*.

What About FX?

Whether you convert your midi tracks to audio with or without FX (effects) is kind of a crap shoot. Either way has its advantages and disadvantages.

If you are in love with the reverb or delay on your midi track you can record a "wet" audio track with your cool FX as part of your sound. However, beware that you are now married to those FX. They cannot be taken off of an audio file.

If, on the other hand, you record your tracks "dry" (without any FX) you will obviously have a choice of FX, compression and limiting at a later date.

I prefer to record them dry and if I am in love with my FX I simply create a document file and write down the details of the exact settings and software I used to achieve my wondrous results. Or, I can record two audio tracks for each instrument – one dry and the other wet with my beloved FX.

Rogaine

These days I am opting to convert all of my midi tracks into audio tracks both for safety and for flexibility reasons - and to keep me from ever again losing a TV placement simply because I cannot successfully remix a song. It is not a pretty sight to see me yelling uncontrollably at a computer screen while simultaneously pulling my hair out.

I am already losing enough hair without hastening the process.

Virtual Instruments and Golf Clubs

It was AWESOME.

It was incredible.

It was one of the most amazing days of my life!

I was so overjoyed I think I even did one of those sprinkler-man victory dances. You know the one, that obnoxious, left hand behind the head, right arm pointing out thing that football players used to do in the end zone after scoring a touchdown.

Yeah, that was me.

New Clubs

It all started when an old acquaintance of mine called to ask if I wanted to go shoot a round of golf with him. He knew I had played the game a little at one time in my life and he also knew that I wasn't particularly good. (Although, I did spend one summer learning the game from a pro and managed to get just good enough so as not to completely embarrass myself.)

I said yes to my friend and we set a tee-off date for the following morning.

I didn't have any golf clubs at the time. Raising three daughters had taken up most of my leisure activity hours and I had given away my clubs. No problem. I would just go down to the local thrift store and pick up some "new" clubs.

Thrift Stores

I headed out to a large thrift store near my house in Seattle, parked my car and walked in. Have you ever be inside a thrift store? They have this smell that is.... how shall I say it? *Unique*. There is nothing quite like it. If you have never been inside a thrift store I strongly suggest you give it a try sometime.

As I strolled through the store toward the back wall, resisting all of the tremendous and tempting deals in my path, I was stung by the buzz of an old familiar feeling – a competitive swell in my gut. I could feel those old juices flowing in a way I had not felt since I started having children and pretty much gave up sports. I liked it. I soon found the section of the store where they had all of their broken down, used sports gear. Just my luck, they had an entire bin filled with an odd array of mismatched golf clubs. It didn't take too much rummaging before I pieced together my makeshift set.

I found the necessities; a putter, the 3, 5, 7 and 9 irons, a couple of woods and a musty old ragged bag. I was set. I took my new found treasure up to the check stand and twenty bucks later I was ready for the Masters.

Unbeknownst to me at the time the real reason my friend wanted to play golf was that he had just purchased a swanky new set of shiny pro clubs for a couple thousand bucks and he wanted to show them off. In retrospect I am fairly certain he also intended to humiliate me with his superior game thereby claiming the undisputed title of "My Life is Better Than Your Life" and in doing so soundly solidify my status (at least in his mind) as a true social inferior – a meager pauper – one of the little people.

Heh.

The Course

I'll keep this short and sweet. The next day we tee'd off, he with his Rolls Royce clubs and me with my Billy Bojangles bag. He knew after just the first few strokes that I had him.

Stroke by stroke, green by green, hole after hole, until all eighteen were played out - it was my day. My lowly, vagabond, twenty dollar clubs had out-witted, out-smarted and out-played his Mr. Mercedes game at every turn, every twist, every sand trap and every green.

I almost felt bad for him.

Almost.

Did I tell you I took private lessons from a pro golfer one summer?

Well, it wasn't so much that - I'm still a way below average golfer - as it was him thinking that his top of the line clubs would somehow magically transform him into a great player.

Virtually Bad

I tell you this because time and time again in the music recording world I hear composers' and producers' songs that have the very latest and greatest virtual instrument samples on them. I mean these guys and girls have spent thousands upon thousands of dollars on their *gear* but the tracks still sound pretty much - I hate to say it - sub-par.

They seem to get just a tad bit irritated when they ask me about my latest TV cue placement and I tell them that the drums, bass and keyboards were all played and recorded using seven-year-old virtual instrument software.

Don't get me wrong, I think some of the new virtual instruments are absolutely fantastic. But I've also heard many composers using virtual instruments that are seven or eight years old and their tracks sound undeniably GREAT. Why? Because - *it's not the gear it's the ear*. There is simply no substitute for taking the gear you already own and learning how to make it sing – how to make it move and groove – how to make it sound wonderful.

There is nothing that will illuminate your flaws more conclusively than recording music using some of these brand new incredible sounding virtual instruments and not fully knowing how to articulate them. A great instrument sample articulated poorly is *glaringly* obvious.

I would guess most any virtual instrument you may have purchased in the last seven or eight years is good enough if you learn how to use it. And those brand new incredible sounding virtual instruments will not sound incredible at all unless you dig in deep and truly learn how to make them realistic.

Quick and Easy

There is no quick and easy way to make your music sound great. Don't fall for the myth that ten thousand dollars worth of the new virtual instruments will suddenly make you sound like a world class composer. Do not make me come over there and snag victory from you with my twenty dollar clubs – or my seven year old samples.

I may, indeed, buy some new golf clubs. (I just spent a few G's on some new virtual instrument horns.) But much more important than new clubs is continuing to practice my swing, my stroke and my mental game, otherwise I'll be standing on the green at the eighteenth hole while someone else does that obnoxious sprinkler-man victory dance....

Go ahead - buy some new stuff if you like.

But don't forget to practice, practice, practice.

Blackberry Cobbler - Templates

If you are contemplating making your career in music production you will need to know that sometimes there are deadlines and you must develop the ability to create and produce your music *very quickly*.

Like overnight.

There have been many times where I have only had a few short hours to start, complete and deliver a piece of music to a client.

This need for speed has happened to me in the TV world, in the advertising industry and elsewhere. One time I was asked to write, record and deliver a potential theme song for a new TV show – literally overnight! (I delivered it on time - but didn't get the gig.)

You win a few, you lose a few.

Learning to produce quality music *quickly* will help you to win a few more and lose a few less.

This makes me want to tell you about my blackberry cobbler.

Blackberry Cobbler

It is no secret around my house that I love blackberry cobbler. I especially love it in the summertime when I can pick the wild blackberries growing around our neighborhood.

A few years ago I began searching for the perfect cobbler recipe. I tried all sorts of recipes. Each time I would try out a new recipe I'd slowly, meticulously and carefully measure out each ingredient, mixing them together precisely per their instructions and then double and triple check each little detail so I could make *thee* perfect cobbler.

If I made one little mistake or cooked it at the wrong temperature, or too slowly, or too fast, it wouldn't turn out perfectly.

My daughters would laugh at me spending twice as long in the kitchen as they did especially when their baking concoctions always turned out better than mine.

After months of experimenting I finally settled on a very simple recipe. It calls for one cup of flour, one third cup of brown sugar, one tablespoon of sugar and one third of a cup of butter at room temperature. (The butter *at room temperature* part is very important. Don't ask me why – I am not a chemist or physicist. It just is.) You spread this concoction over your blackberry mix and bake it for precisely 25 minutes at 400 degrees.

As with all of the other recipes I experimented with I spent a good thirty minutes slowly double and triple checking the details making sure I had it down. Making sure that the oven was set just right, that I had the pan on the middle rack, that the oven was pre-heated and that the timer was set to go off in twenty-five minutes *exactly*.

Now that I have made this particular blackberry cobbler dozens and dozens of times I can put it together in about ten minutes and it turns out *perfectly* – every time. But it did take quite a bit of practice doing it slowly and double checking everything to get it down.

There is also, of course, the additional skill of getting just the exact amount of French Vanilla ice cream spread out over the top in just the right way. Then as it starts to melt – your timing has to be perfect - you dig in. I have become an expert at this craft as well. It is heaven.

So why am I telling you this stuff about blackberry cobblers?

Templates

When I first started recording instrumental cues for film and TV it would take me 20 to 25 hours to complete a cue. Now it takes me between 4 and 8 hours to write and complete a production depending upon length and complexity of the style.

So how did I go from an average of 22.5 hours down to an average of about 6 hours per production? It has a lot to do with building *templates*.

Back when I was just beginning to learn my cue craft I would spend hours upon hours listening to each individual kick drum sound in my virtual instrument library, every snare drum sound, the hi-hat sounds, and on down the line. I would try out 15 or 20 basses trying to find just the right one.

I did the same thing for organ sounds, piano sounds, string patches, guitar amps and, well, every instrument that went into producing the cue. I would spend hours measuring out the specific *ingredients* to make the tastiest recipe.

And not really knowing how to produce the perfect track I had to try out a lot of different recipes to figure out what I was doing and then try get better at it.

But, slowly, after recording cues number two, three, four, fifteen through fifty, I started to find out that some of the same ingredients, some particular basses and certain guitar sounds, kick drums and every other instrument, made for the tastiest cobblers – the best music – every time.

I began to realize that whatever style of music I was producing, be it AOR or Pop or Hip-Hop (or whatever), there were specific instrument sounds that worked best for each genre. Just like some ingredients work best for a blackberry cobbler and others work best for a pepperoni pizza – so it is with music.

I then began to build templates of my discoveries for each particular genre I produced.

If I am producing a Nashville Country cue I know that my drums are going to be one of just a couple drum kits. I also know that there are two or three basses that work best for me in that genre almost every time.

I have learned (for example) that when I am playing a smooth jazz guitar part for a Muzak track I am most likely going to use the bass pickups on my Fender Strat and start with the Line 6 POD setting 4A as my beginning point for a guitar sound - that is, if I don't go straight to the Archtop.

I am creating templates - or recipes - for each style of music I produce.

In other words, practice, experimentation and learning what works and what does not work will make your cobblers more delicious and your cues more quickly "in the pocket."

Abundance

Do you see what I am getting at? I had to ask the questions, research the desserts and then experiment with various ingredients in order to discover the best cobbler recipe. And when I finally found the perfect combination it became my *template* for further successes.

Has having production templates in my recording studio made me better music producer?

Absolutely! And they have also made me able to much more quickly achieve whatever it is I have set out to accomplish.

Templates are a sure-fire way to get your cues done well and quickly. They can also simply be a starting point, a jumping off point, the beginning of a new path you may forge in pursuit of your own original art.

Example Template

Here is an example template of a straight-ahead, pop-rock cue using mostly virtual instruments and a couple "real" guitar tracks. In this example I am working with some *really* old software as well as some newer virtual instrument software.

* Kick – SampleTank2/Drums/Acoustic/BD, E3 (trim Decay back to 100)
* Hi-Hat – SampleTank2, A4
* Snare – EZdrummer – Nashville expansion kit (use EZdrummer room reverb)
* Toms – EZdrummer – Nashville expansion kit (use EZdrummer room reverb)
* Crashes – (Either EZ or ST2)
* Bass – SampleTank2, P-Bass (fingered), back tone down to 4.2 (go to Trilogy if necessary)
* Acoustic Piano – SampleTank2/Bright Concert Piano KW (add a touch of high end EQ and ST2 reverb 21% - 2.4 sec.)
* Percussion – (if tambourine, use ST2/percussion/tambourine, if Claps – use ST2/Drums/Electronic/800)
* Guitar 1 – Fender Strat through Pod (maybe start with Pod preset 2B)
* Guitar 2 – Fender Strat either doubling guitar 1 with different settings and/or chord/fret placements, or record add additional new guitar part
* Guitar 3 – Omnisphere/Vintage/Strat (or other)
* Chorus pad – Omnisphere/Human Voices/Pop stack/male &female/aahs or oos/ 25% Omnisphere rvb)
* High string pad – SampleTank2/Synth/Pad/Beyond Voyage
* Additional "glue" pad or El. Piano (wherever can help glue the track together)
* Pan most drums and bass straight-up 12 o'clock

* Pan Acoustic piano just off center and left at about 11:00 to 11:20
* Pan... spread everything else out to taste
* Set FX and levels to personal taste
* Mix using slight amount of limiting or compression
* Master with Ozone 3 – CD Mastering or other settings (set to taste)

This is just one of an infinite amount of templates I have discovered. This particular template enables me to produce a two minute pop-rock instrumental cue in 4 to 6 hours.

Happy templating!

Accentuate the Positive (Recording the Vocalist)

I've got a few questions for you.

Has anyone ever made you angry?

Has anyone ever criticized or said something really rude to you?

Maybe it was your boss, maybe your boyfriend, your girlfriend or your spouse.

Have you ever overheard someone gossiping about you or read a maliciously unflattering post about yourself on Facebook or another web site?

Most of us have experienced some kind of disrespect at one time or another in our life.

Let me ask you this: When someone disrespected you, how did it make you feel?

Did your blood boil? Did steam come out your ears? Did your heart rate rise, your face get hot and your throat tighten? Did it make you feel hurt and alone? Did you want to cry?

Think back to when you were a kid in school. Were you ever bullied or teased by any of the other kids? Did you ever find yourself embarrassed by something you did or something someone *said* you did?

How did you feel in that moment?

I once shot at the wrong basket in an eighth grade basketball game. The wrong basket! In front of a thousand people! In *eighth grade*! Do you know how emotionally vulnerable an eighth grader is? I wanted to crawl into a hole. I wanted to die. I tried everything I could to never have to go back to school again. The whole embarrassing incident made me physically ill. I struggled to hide my tears as my mother told me that I absolutely had to go back to school and face the music. It was devastating.

Chemicals

Most of us have experienced the unpleasant physical sensations that come along with being totally embarrassed, frustrated, hurt or angry. When we have a negative reaction to an event a bunch of chemicals are released into our body's system that actually cause very real and sometimes extreme physical symptoms. Researchers have proven beyond a shadow of any doubt that our psychological state does indeed affect our physical state.

Doctors have known for years that an intense anxiety response to an event will trigger a release of adrenaline into our system subsequently triggering a truck load of other chemical reactions which are also released into our body's highways. Physical symptoms such as raising blood pressure levels, sweating, heart racing, fainting, loss of digestive function and many others can occur.

Even mildly anxious moments can produce some very dramatic physical changes in us. Tightness or thickening of the throat, a nauseous feeling, light-headedness, heart palpitations, shakiness etc...

The Vocalist

The reason I am telling you this is because a singer's physical instrument is part of this very same emotional, electro-chemical highway. When we are recording a vocalist we need to be aware that our words - how we coach them or steer them toward desired results - will make all the difference in the world between getting a great track and messing up the entire session.

Certainly all great musicians play their instruments with intense emotion. This is exactly what we want from any musician - an emotional performance as opposed to a purely mechanical performance. But instrumentalists and vocalists are somewhat different. When we tell a saxophone player that his performance sucks, he may be emotionally set back but his actual instrument, his saxophone, will not have been affected at all.

However, when we tell a vocalist that the song they just sang stunk, not only do we affect them emotionally but we have altered the very physical structure of their instrument. Their vocal chords, their diaphragm and their breathing are no longer functioning in a way conducive to giving a great performance.

It is very possible to utterly destroy a vocalist's instrument with just a few unkind words. We, as producers, must develop the skill of a psychologist if we want to get the best from our vocalists. If we do not implement a positive approach we may, indeed, find them performing with a damaged instrument much like a guitar player trying to perform with two broken guitar strings or a drummer playing on a torn snare head.

Accentuate the Positive

I have found that with a little practice we can always frame our advice or coaching in a positive way. Here is an example.

Walk with me for a moment out to the front yard and garden of my house.

If someone comes over to my home and makes a remark about my garden and landscaping, which of the two following comments do you think I will respond to in a positive way:

"Your garden looks horrible with all of those weeds in it."

Or...

"I love the color of your dahlias and you have found the perfect spot for those cute petunias - they are beautiful. I'd love to come over and work with you in your garden sometime."

It's a no brainer, right? The first comment is framed in the negative and would probably upset me. The person delivering the second comment may want to come over and work in my garden because they also think it looks terrible but because they have framed their remarks in the positive I would be quite receptive to their offer. And feel good about it.

If a vocalist is not heading in the direction you want, simply compliment them on how cool they sound (they probably *do* sound cool), tell them you're going to keep that particular track and then ask them if they'd mind, just for fun, trying a couple of different approaches - just to see what it sounds like.

Give them a good example of the vibe you would like and then open up a new track and have at it. If you are correct in the approach you are directing them toward, the new tracks will sound better. And when you play back the new vocals they will actually *hear* the difference and you can build positively from there.

The Other Side of the Coin

Years and years ago before my brother had his record deal and his hit songs, a producer friend of mine and I had him come into my little demo studio to see if we could get a great vocal track out of him. We ended up doing about 80 punch-ins or retakes of his vocal track that day - on one song. I was not yet skilled in the psychological aspect of producing a vocalist and neither was my producer friend.

We pushed him hard - real hard. And we weren't very tactful in our coaching or advice. We got a good track that day but my brother will tell you that after he left that session he sat in his car for a long, long time, absolutely crushed by our sledgehammer approach and contemplated quitting the music business altogether. A handful of hit songs and two record deals later I'm glad he didn't quit.

My brother will also tell you that a few days later when he got up the courage to listen to the song we had recorded, he realized it was the best his vocals had ever sounded - so it gave him some hope. Harsh as it was he would call me years later thanking me for that experience because the producers in Nashville were pushing him even harder and farther.

My brother is tough - in a good way. If you want to be a professional recording vocalist you absolutely have to be tough. If you are not, you will be eaten alive by the continual judgments of others. Note to vocalists: *Grow a thick skin*!

I tell you this not because I think the sledgehammer approach will get a better vocal - it usually will *not* get you a better vocal. I tell you this because we were very lucky that our heavy handed approach didn't kill my brother's musical career that day.

During that session, when we recorded my brother those many years ago, we probably would have gotten an *even better* vocal if we had framed our coaching in the positive instead of the negative and we wouldn't have run the risk of destroying his career by being jerks.

Life

Believe me, you will get better results from your vocalists if you can simply learn to frame your advice in the positive.

This, too, is an important *life* skill. Learn to frame all of your relationship words in the positive and your relationships will be stronger, you will be at peace, and successes will magically follow you wherever you go.

Accentuate the positive.

Note: This above reality of vocalist recording is one of the main reasons why smart engineers and producers always record the vocalist while they are getting a mic check and doing a *run-through*. When the vocalists are just warming up, the pressure is off, no critiques have yet been made and sometimes they will give their best performance simply because they are having fun with the track. Often they will flat out *sing* the song during a mic check - instead of trying to sing it the way they *think* they should.

Takeaways (Chapters 6 – 10)

1. Use real instruments (along with virtual instruments) for more realism in your cues.

2. Convert your midi tracks to audio tracks.

3. Convert midi to audio dry (without FX) if possible.

4. Make certain to log all of you FX settings when converting midi to audio dry. (For easy recall)

5. Learn your gear. Great sounding Virtual Instruments only sound good if you know how to use them.

6. Study all of your Virtual Instruments and build templates for different genres.

7. Templates help you become faster at producing music.

8. Poorly chosen words can have a negative effect on a singer's performance.

9. Frame all of your remarks to the vocalist (and other musicians)

in the positive.

10. Vocalists (and all musicians) must strive to grow a thick skin and to take criticism in a professional manner.

11. It is smart to record the vocalist while they are warming up and doing a run through. This is often when you will get their most relaxed and optimum performance.

How I Record My Guitar

I almost didn't write this chapter.

Why?

Because I don't really consider myself a great guitar player.

My main instrument is piano.

But then I got to thinking.

I *do* play a lot of guitar on a lot of recordings. And those recordings get played on a lot of TV shows. Maybe I have at least a little something to offer.

Still, it needs to be said that I personally know many, many guitar players who can play circles around me. And I hire a few of them from time to time to play certain parts and styles that are not my strong suit.

So there you have it - my guitar playing disclaimer.

In my guitar playing defense, however, let me offer a summation about the kind of guitar player I consider myself to be (at least in my own delusional mind):

I don't play the most notes - I just play the best notes.

Having Fun

Undoubtedly, my very favorite way to record my own guitar playing is when there is no project due, no time constraints, no rush to meet any deadlines - just hours and hours of free and open creative space laying in front of me.

Unfortunately, I usually *do* have a deadline to meet which means I rarely get to record the guitar my favorite way.

When I am recording my electric guitar I most often use my Fender Stratocaster. It is nothing to brag about really, just a mainline Strat which is always patiently waiting in the corner of my studio for a chance to do its thing.

While I prefer to use the Fender Strat I really could be using any decent guitar with good pickups. I have also used a Les Paul, a Tele, a couple Archtops and many others for recording. Each guitar is cool and has its own unique strengths and weaknesses. Since they all have different sounds I suggest you always use the guitar that best allows you to achieve the specific sounds you are looking for.

The Luxury of Time

When I have all of the time in the world at my disposal I like to experiment with mic settings and natural reverb. I usually use my old (circa early 70s) Fender Vibrosonic amp which has one fifteen inch JBL speaker in it.

Most often when I am recording my Strat I am alone in the studio overdubbing my parts. Being the only player in the room gives me a great deal of freedom in where I place my mics. If I were recording with a band I would have the natural constraints that come with other musician's instruments bleeding into my guitar mics. But recording the guitar separately against a pre-recorded band track gives me unlimited flexibility in microphone experimentation.

I will quite often put my Vibrosonic amp in the garage to take advantage of the concrete reverb reflections just to see if I can come up with something amazing. I will almost always put one mic - usually an old Sure SM58 - on the edge of the speaker cone pointed inwards toward the center of the speaker and about an inch or so away from the grill-cloth. This gives me that wonderful "in your face" tight guitar sound that is always the meat of my track.

After I have the close-mic set up I will put another mic about five feet away and either point it toward the amp or away from the amp. Pointing it toward the amp can give me additional depth in my guitar sound and pointing it away will record more of the sound reflections that I will use for a possible room reverb effect. I will then send the signal from this mic to its own track in my DAW. (Note that I have sent the signal from the *close* mic to its own separate track as well.)

Giving each mic signal its own separate track in my DAW means I will be able to retain my guitar mixing options for a later time. I want to do this because it gives me the greatest flexibility in molding and shaping my guitar part to best enhance the song and fit perfectly with the other instruments in the mix.

I may also set up a third mic that is just outside of the room to record the sound of the room that is being pushed out through the door. I will put this mic on a third separate track for additional natural reverb or delay options.

I may not end up using all three mics - often I do not - but each additional microphone recording my guitar on its own separate track will give me more and more options for mixing. And as I have said, I have all of the time in the world when I am recording this way, so why not experiment a little.

As you may already be able to tell the options for mic placement are limitless. Heck, you can set up a mic on the top of your home studio's roof dangling down the chimney with a fire burning and record that if you want to. Although I find that it always works better when you do not have a raging fire in your fireplace.

If I haven't mentioned it already I will always try to record my guitar "dry" with no FX so that I may retain full FX options later in the mix.

Mix

After I have recorded my guitar part I now have three tracks to work with: the close mic track, the five-feet-back mic track and the track of the mic just outside of the room. I usually start my mix by getting the close mic's track to sound perfect with the other two mic's track faders pulled down. If I have done my job right and adjusted my guitar and amp to sound cool **before** I have recorded them, then I have very little EQ-ing to do.

Once I have my close-miked track sounding good and beefy I will start easing in one or the other of the room mics. This experimentation of mic-track combinations can go on for quite a while as I listen for that "magic" - that guitar sound that makes me go "wow!" There is no real formula for mixing these tracks together. The whole idea in this type of recording is discovery through experimentation.

I know my guitar track mix is right when it sounds *freaking great.*

Note that you do not want to change any of your guitar, amp or mic placement settings until you are certain you have recorded what you needed. Going back at a later date and trying to set everything up again in the exact same way in order to fix a part is, well, basically impossible.

Deadlines

About 90% of my guitar recording projects have time constraints and deadlines. Sometimes I only have an hour or so to get it right and get it down on tape. (Sorry, I'm old school and still call it "tape." I should probably have said "get it down digitally," but saying it that way still feels wrong to me.)

When I do not have the luxury of time and experimentation I will often bypass using an amplifier and any microphones altogether. I simply plug my electric guitar into my Line 6 POD, send the signal out through a preamp and into my DAW and then have at it.

The lengthiest part of this particular type of setup is tuning the guitar.

I have been using my Strat and POD combination for so long I usually know what two or three presets will be good starting points for any particular song or cue style. Once I have found my preset I will tweak it until I find the perfect sound and then hit record.

Even when using the POD or some similar device there can be a lot of experimentation but my purposes for using this combination are simple: It sounds pretty darn good and I can get my guitar parts recorded fast.

Depending on what kind of guitar part I am playing I will often double it (play it twice with each performance recorded on a separate track). Especially if it is a chunky chord part. When I double my guitar I will not use the exact same settings on each guitar track. I will either use a different POD sound or pickup setting, or I will play a different inversion of the same chord for each individual track. I may pan the two tracks hard left and right and tuck them back (lower their volume) in the mix. This doubling process can have wonderful results in making my guitar sound *bigger*.

Sometimes, when I want that *huge* rock guitar sound, I will play and record the same part as many as four times – each time recording the new guitar part on separate a track and each with unique guitar settings or inversions.

I use this technique mostly when I am recording power rock tracks. This approach can give you a monstrous sound, but the more guitar tracks you play and record of the same guitar part, the tighter they must be played. Nothing will cause you to lose your instrument's punch and bite more quickly than four tracks that are all attacking and releasing at slightly different times. Your power track can become a pile of mush if you don't pay particular attention to your accuracy and consistency.

I have indeed created some mush at times by getting in a hurry and not paying close enough attention to performance detail. All I can really do then is trash it all and start over.

The Guitar Part

I must also add that there have been many times with both of these recording processes where I have found what I would call the **killer** guitar sound and yet somehow after I record my part and then listen back, it doesn't sound good at all.

In most of these cases it wasn't that my actual guitar *sound* was bad, it was that my guitar *part* was very mediocre. The notes, rhythms and chords I had been playing were either sub-par or not quite right for the particular song I was recording. And these mediocre guitar parts were tricking my ear into thinking the guitar's *sound* stunk up the joint.

In these sessions as soon as I take a little time and come up with a better guitar **part,** the sound of my guitar magically and mysteriously resurrects itself.

Thirty Seconds

An additional cool thing about recording in the studio is that I only have to be a great musician for about 30 seconds at a time. This is about the length of an average song's verse or chorus. Once I have my thirty seconds sounding good I can simply stop the recording and regroup my thoughts for the next 30-second section.

Since many verses and choruses have the same recurring guitar parts I can often just get one verse down and then copy and paste it to the second verse section in my DAW. The same process of copy and paste can often be used for the choruses as well.

Many guitar and engineer purists hate this process. They want you to play the whole song from top to bottom. I guess I'm not a purist. Oh darn.

The way I see it, if Leonardo Da Vinci would have had access to Photoshop for his paintings he probably would have used it. He was an artist but also an innovator taking advantage of all of the latest technology of his day. As I recall, he even invented some new technology that wouldn't come to fruition until hundreds of years after his death.

Imagine – the Mona Lisa Photoshopped. How dare I suggest such a thing!

The Acoustic

Recording an acoustic guitar is much the same as recording the electric guitar. However, if the acoustic is going to be *naked* - as in a sparse singer-songwriter type track - I must always mic it. I need to be able to hear and feel the wood.

I've tried all of my mics - the Shures, Sennheiser, AKG and Neumann - and they all work well in their own way, each with a different sound or depth. Probably the easiest way for me to get a really good acoustic guitar sound quickly is to put my AKG (C 460 B) about six inches from the body of the guitar pointed somewhere between the bridge and the hole.

That lone mic can work just fine in a lot of instances but I will usually position another mic a foot or two away pointing toward a different part of the guitar and send its signal to a separate track so I can have some depth and flexibility in the acoustic guitar mix.

If I am putting an acoustic guitar part onto a rocking band track and its purpose is mostly for texture and feel I will sometimes use a guitar with a pickup. That way I can simply and quickly run a line into my DI (Direct Input or Direct Box) and then into my board and DAW - and call it good.

I have on occasion recorded my acoustic with a direct line (no mics) and then beefed up its sound by adding a great virtual guitar sample. By doubling the real guitar and playing the exact same guitar notes on my keyboard (triggering a virtual guitar sample) I have sometimes achieved a wonderful sound. When I use this process I get both the *real* feel from my live guitar playing and some unique sound combinations from adding the virtual instrument.

FX

I always try to record my guitar parts whether electric or acoustic absolutely dry with no FX whatsoever. I have sometimes broken my own rule and recorded my guitar with POD FX already attached. However, when I do this I am stuck with what I have. It is impossible to remove reverb or delay or any other processing once it has been recorded as an audio track. The only way to change it is to record the whole shebang all over again.

After my **dry** guitar parts are laid down and I'm feeling good about them there are numerous FX and various processing toys I can apply to achieve my desired effect. I've experimented with hundreds of different processing gizmos and have my favorites. (I have those "go to" processors and settings I know will work well for any particular guitar part in any one of dozens of song styles.)

I'd tell you what they all are but that information is *top secret*. Not really. Actually the best way for you to find out what *your* favorites will be is to experiment and identify which FX you like and which ones will "sit well" in any given music style.

When you are first experimenting with various types of processing it is a good idea to **write down** your favorite FX findings, compression settings, etc... That way you can *recall* what the heck you did on that really cool song you recorded last month. Build a file of song titles and the FX you used and then store that file on your hard drive. I sometimes keep a document of these settings right inside of any giving DAW session's song file.

A Million Ways

There are a million ways to get your guitar to sound cool. I have just given you a few of the ways I like to record and a handful of tricks I use when I need to get a good sound *fast*.

I am at my core still a student, always learning and continually looking for new ways to improve my sound and increase my speed in getting those sounds. The sky's the limit. Go create some brilliant guitar tracks and rock the world, baby!

Guitar Recording Summation

1. Put a close mic near amp speaker and a room mic a few feet away.

2. Send the mic signals to separate DAW tracks.

3. Get the guitar and amp to sound great before recording (per minimal EQ layer).

4. Record the guitar parts dry (no FX) to maximize FX options in the mix.

5. Record all overdubs before changing any setting or mic placements.

6. Double tracking the guitar part can make the sound bigger.

7. If the guitar tracks don't sound good check to see if you have played the best guitar "parts."

8. Copy and paste can speed up the recording process.

9. Record the acoustic guitar with two separate mics (send the mic signals to separate tracks for maximum mix options).

10. Keep an accurate record of all settings logged in the song's file.

Mixing the Bass

Ah, the bass guitar....

Recording and mixing the bass....

My great nemesis.

The Rubik's Cube of recording.

The thrill of victory and the agony of defeat.

Taming the Beast

I must confess I have not yet been able to fully figure out how to tame the beast – to get a glorious mix with the bass guitar, that is. I record bass on over 100 songs or cues per year but I am not sure I have ever been completely satisfied with my results. It is the one instrument where I feel like I am always compromising the sound just a little bit to try to get it to *fit* into the track's mix. When it comes to mixing the bass, *every song is different*.

I have consulted with many Bass Recording Oracles around the globe and although some of them will claim to have discovered "the magic," I have listened to their songs and I can assure you they are compromising quite often too. That elusive, perfect bass sound you hear in a song from time to time seems to have happened more by accident than by design.

Mixing the bass for me is a bit like wearing the suit and tie my wife makes me put on once in awhile when she gets tired of seeing me in T-shirts and blue jeans. It's a good suit, it fits ok, but it never seems to feel quite right when I'm wearing it. I always feel like other people are looking at me as if I just stepped out of a thrift store wearing someone else's threads, shaking their heads in pity at what a bad fit it is and turning away with a disgusted sigh.

I wish I had some magic formula I could share with you that would make your bass mixing easier and your songs truly shine every time. I don't. I have, however, found some things that can help tremendously in solving the bass mixing riddle which I now have stuffed into my bag of tricks.

Steps

One: First and foremost, even before you set foot in a recording studio, the number one thing that will make your bass sound better in the mix is to write a GREAT song. I'm not kidding. Nothing will help the bass sound cooler than a great song to riff under. This first step cannot be stressed enough. A wonderfully written song or a perfectly composed music cue will solve many, many, MANY bass problems.

Two: Write a great *arrangement* for your song. Getting all of the instruments to play the perfect complimentary parts will go a long way in helping everything to sound incredible together.

Three: Get your awesome bass sounds *before* you record. Get them *before* you mic your amp and *before* your count off your tune. Make sure you have a killer sounding bass coming through the amp. Or make certain that you have the perfect sounding virtual instrument sample *before* you do anything else. Also, take note what kind of bass you are using. Is it the right bass for the style of song you are recording?

For example, if you have chosen an upright acoustic bass for a traditional funk song I would suggest you maybe consider making a change. And although using a fretless on a heavy metal song may seem like an artsy thing to do I doubt you will get the results needed for your metal track to compete out there in the hard rocker world.

Also, your sound will be tremendously affected by whether you use a pick or fingers (or teeth) on your strings. The type of bass strings you use (flatwound, roundwound, etc...) will make a big difference too, as will where on the bass you are striking your strings. Pay attention to these types of details *before* you record. It will pay off big time later when you mix.

Four: If you are not a seasoned bass player it is a good idea to get a fantastic professional studio bass player to play on your song. As long as you can communicate your ideas to him or her you won't regret it. Avoid Johnny Wannabe who has yet to play a gig outside of his mom's garage. He may have a cool looking bass but it is doubtful he will bring the goods to the table.

If you are in a band make sure you practice your butt off *before* you begin to record. If you are using samples you can quantize the bass but beware of over-quantizing. Over-quantizing can quickly cause you to lose the human feel in your bass line. There is no substitute for having a rock solid, tightly played part to helping your mix sound great.

Five: Fifth on my list is to take some time and listen to your bass guitar and the kick drum together. Nothing will mush up a mix quicker than a boomy kick drum and a boomy bass both boldly strutting their stuff and proudly pontificating in the same song.

Simply stated, one of them needs to change. If the bass sound you desire is more on the boomy side then make the kick a little crisper – or vice versa. The possibilities here are limitless. You need to experiment until you have the perfect sounding combination of kick drum and bass.

Six: Watch out for other low frequency instruments in your song. A low droning synthesizer or the low end of stacked guitars can often compete with (and for) the bass frequencies in your mix. You may need to change a synthesizer or guitar part to make them better sing with your bass.

It should be noted here that in most any song a good rule of thumb for all of the instruments and arrangements as well as for the songwriting is: less is usually more. Usually when you play and write less stuff your song gets *bigger*. The reverse is true as well. Often when you play and write more notes your song will get smaller.

I know this is a difficult thing to do. We all spend years and years learning how to play lots of notes and how to play them fast only to have some record producer tell us to play less. But no one said it was gonna be easy to make brilliant music. Indeed, quite often, less IS more. Except for those rare times when more is more – more or less. Never mind. We'll get to that later.

Seven: Don't put any crap on your bass. Record it clean with no FX, no unnecessary EQ and no compression if possible. All that stuff can be added later but can't be *taken away*. (I always recommend keeping the add-ons to a bare minimum on bass even after it is recorded.) If you record a bass with heavy reverb and phase it may be impossible to get it to sit into the mix later on down the road. If you record it "dry" then you retain the option of dabbing bits of goo upon its dryness later if so desired. The same rule holds true when you are using samples and recording your bass as a midi track. You will have more flexibility if you record the bass as clean as possible.

Eight: If I am using samples I will often try out a couple different bass "sounds." It is a good idea to choose a couple different bass guitar samples and try each one in the track to see if magic happens. If I have used a fingered P-Bass in my original track I might try a J-Bass or a P-Bass with a pick, or any one of a number of other options just to see if some new bass takes the song in a cool new direction and *sits* better with the other instruments.

If you are playing live bass with a band in the studio it is a real good idea to have your bass completely isolated just in case you need to over-dub a different bass or fix a bass part after the band has laid down an otherwise perfect track.

Nine: Begin your mix. I usually put the bass and kick straight up, 12 o'clock center (panning) but you can try to pan them wherever you want. You'll probably end up with them at 12 o'clock but one of the ways you learn this is to try them everywhere and see what they sound like. So have some fun and experiment.

As I am beginning my mix I will also have a couple of songs from major artists handy that I can use as reference tracks to see if my mixes are in the ball park with the big boys. If I am recording a country-pop track I may have a Keith Urban song handy. If I am working on heavy rock I might have a Metallica track nearby for reference. I will try to find major artist songs that are not only in the same genre but have the same *feel* as my song. The idea here is this: major artists have spent hundreds of thousands of dollars hiring the best songwriters, engineers, musicians, producers and mastering engineers to create a world class product. It benefits us to use those experts' recordings as templates for our own production, mixing and mastering.

This is where your cars come in. Does the bass you just mixed sit in the pocket as well as Keith Urban's bass? If not, why? Is it too hot, too quiet? Is it too boomy or too thin? Does it have enough growl or edge or is it lacking bite? Is the actual bass part wrong? Do you need record the bass again playing another line?

Your ear will be your guide but using songs by a Major Artist as your mixing template (for all instruments) will help you achieve your desired results.

Ten: Remember, *everything affects everything*. Be cognizant that when you change the lead vocal in the mix or the guitar sound or its placement in the mix it will affect your bass. You may have your bass sitting perfectly in the mix but after you add a little more delay to the lead vocal and pan the electric guitars a little farther to the left and right, your bass may no longer be working as well in the mix. You will need to adjust it. Get out your reference tracks and repeat step nine.

Eleven: After you think you have achieved the perfect mix you can move on to the final step - number 11. Now is the time to burn a copy of your mix and then listen to it on a variety of systems outside of your studio. I listen to my cues on my living room stereo, my office computer speakers and on the media system in my Jeep. They are all very different sounding stereo systems. If my mix sounds great on *all* of those systems, I am done. It is finished. If I hear something wacky with the bass, as often happens, I need to identify it, go back into my studio, fix it, run off a new mix and then repeat step eleven.

You are now done. Your bass sounds incredible. Your mix sparkles like a Grammy winner and you are just a few weeks away from making millions of dollars.

Bass Mix Summation

1. Write a great song.

2. Write a great song arrangement.

3. Get great sounds for all of your instruments before you record.

4. Use great players or practice your butt off until you can play your instrument well.

5. Analyze the Bass and Kick.

6. Watch out for any low frequency instruments that may conflict with your bass.

7. Don't booger up your bass with too many FX.

8. Experiment with different basses or bass samples.

9. Use reference tracks while mixing in the same style as your song.

10. Remember, everything affects everything.

11. Test your mix on multiple systems.

There you have it - straight from the horse's hoof.

If there is a better way to mix the bass, I want to know about it.

Mixing the bass is, after all, my greatest nemesis.

Pushing Air - Big Sound

So, you say you want that BIG studio sound.

You want your recordings to sound HUGE...

You want them to explode out of the speakers like the mixes the pros get in their multi-million dollar recording studios.

But you are using mostly virtual instruments.

You like the way your virtual instruments sound but no matter how well you articulate them they just don't have the same punch or realism that the big boys toys have.

"What is their trick?" You ask. "How do I make my virtual instruments sound real, cool and BIG in my home studio?"

The answer is easy – push air.

Pushing Air

Back in the old days of recording when there were no virtual instruments, when real players played real instruments, those instruments were miked. The instrument's sound either came out of a natural instrument, like a horn which was miked or it came through the speakers of an amplifier – which was also miked. Either way they were *pushing air* with sound.

If you had an electric guitar plugged into an amplifier you were pushing air out of the amp's speaker and into a couple of microphones. If you were recording a non-amped instrument like vocals or a saxophone you were pushing air out of the instrument or vocalist's mouth and into a microphone.

Virtual instruments on the other hand push no air. Sure, some of them sound fabulous and have been created to emulate air being pushed but they are not actually *pushing air*.

This diminishes their capacity to sound real or *really big*.

Pushing air matters.

Tripping

You can, however, make your virtual instruments push air.

How?

Take them on a trip.

You can take your virtual instruments on a trip either while you are recording them or send them on a journey *after* you have recorded them to a track. To take your VI's on a trip you simply need to send the VI's signal to an amplifier and from the amp to a speaker. Once the instrument's sound is coming out of the speaker you can mic it and record your new "pushing air" sound on an audio track in your DAW.

Yes, this is an additional step in your recording process but even if you only do it with a couple of virtual instruments you will notice your recorded sounds getting more *real*. Doing this will help you better achieve that big studio sound you have been longing to create.

Even Drums?

You can do this process with any virtual instrument - even drums. For example: Isolate your pre-recorded virtual snare drum track and send it out through an amp to a speaker. Then mic and record the snare sound *pushing air* through the amp's speaker. Send that amp's mic signal to a new audio track in your DAW and presto! Do the same trick with the kick, toms and the rest of the drum kit. And while you are at it, send your virtual bass through an amp and mic its speaker as well.

This process gives you the additional advantage of adding a second mic and using your room's natural reverb to enhance your sound.

Go ahead. Give it a try.

Experiment with different amps and different microphones to see what works best for you.

Recording may take a little longer but your sound will get a lot bigger.

Takeaways

1. Push air for a bigger sound
2. Send virtual instruments through miked speaker to an audio track on your DAW

Panning: Where do I put Lead Vocals and other Instruments?

Before you mix (heck, before you record), there are a few things you need to do that will make the difference between your mix being good and sucking.

Let me offer some pre-mixing suggestions.

(I mentioned some of these things in the "Mixing the Bass" chapter. I am listing them again because they apply to overall mixing as well as to the bass.)

The most important thing to remember is that you need to get your song written well and sounding cool *before* you record. This holds true for instrumental cues as well. You need to have a pretty good idea of where the track is heading before you press the record button. (There are of course some music cue producers who write and arrange *as they record*. Most, however, who are successful at simultaneously writing and recording have hundreds if not thousands of cues already under their belt.)

The other most important thing you need to do is to get your arrangement and instrument parts right – at least in your head - *before* you record. In addition, make sure all of your players and singers are not just good - but *great* - or at least as great and well-rehearsed as possible. Again, this is something you need to do *before* you record.

You will also need to get all of the musicians' instruments sounding great *before* you record and *before* you ever put a mic on them or their amps. (I.e. the drums need to be tuned up and the amps, guitars, keyboards and bass need to have some awesome sounds coming out of them *prior* to recording.)

The last thing you need to do is to get a clean, dry-as-possible signal from your instrument and vocal sounds onto tape - *recorded digitally* - without getting in their way.

Don't goober up the sounds with FX until after they have been recorded.

If you have done all of these things then you should be able to get a good mix fairly easily.

Planning the Panning

In this section I am not going to talk about EQ, compression and FX (just remember, less is more). I am simply going to give you a map or template of instrument and vocal placement (panning) that will work quite well for all of the pop, rock and country mainstream radio genres. Remember this is just a map, a guideline to help make your mixes sound really good. These are not hard and fast rules. Some of the coolest music ever made veers from these guidelines.

I will use the image of an old circular "clock" to make panning suggestions for each instrument.

OK here we go. Here is a typical popular music panning mix.

* Lead vocal - 12 o'clock, noon.
* Kick - 12 o'clock
* Snare - 12' o'clock
* Bass guitar - 12 o'clock

* Hi-hat - 1 o'clock or 11 o'clock
* Crash and ride cymbals - 1 o'clock and 11 o'clock
* Toms - You can spread them out a bit between 10 and 2 o'clock
* Electric rhythm guitar(s) x2 - put one guitar at 3 o'clock and the other at 9 o'clock.
* Piano - 10:45 (almost 11 o'clock)
* Organ or Synthesizer - 1:15 to 1:30 (o'clock)
* Any lead instrument: keep it close to 12 o'clock as long as it doesn't conflict with the lead vocal.
* Background vocals - just off center - 11:30 or 12:30
* Pads and strings - tricky - sometimes I'll pan one far left at about 8 o'clock and balance it with another pad at 4 o'clock although sometimes a track calls for me to sneak them in almost anywhere.
* Percussion - if I pan some percussion left, I will try to find its counterpart (another instrument) to pan right for balance.

Stereo

I'm not a huge fan of stereo instruments in the mix (I.e. having the same guitar part coming out of both left and right speakers) simply because when I am watching a band perform live on stage in a small venue the guitar player's sound is usually coming from one direction as is every other instrument.

However, in a large arena you would hear every instrument coming from just about everywhere. So if you want your mix to sound like a large, 10,000 seat arena just put a bunch of reverb and delay on everything and have all of the instruments coming out of every speaker. This way you will achieve that "rock concert" sound, with everyone's instrument bouncing off of the concrete walls and ceilings. And it will sound like crap.

Having said that, I do from time to time mix a guitar part or a pad in stereo (both left and right). If done on the right instruments at the right time it can, indeed, be cool and help give that often desired *bigness* to your song.

If you start panning your mix using the map above as a guideline I am fairly certain you will achieve a pretty good panning mix of your song.

Panning Summary

1. Vocals and instruments will always sound better if the song is well written.

2. Make certain your arrangement is great before you record.

3. Use the best musicians possible.

4. Get all of the instruments sounding great *before* you record them.

5. Record all tracks with a dry-as-possible signal.

6. Panning in stereo can give certain parts a bigger sound.

7. Pan lead vocal, snare, kick and bass guitar straight up 12 o'clock.

8. Mirror each type of instrument panned left with its counterpart panned right.

The Arrangement (Don't Forget About It)

I heard a new song the other day from a producer friend of mine.

The song had a string orchestra in it which sounded fantastic.

I was particularly interested in what sample library he used for his strings because I am currently working on some string orchestra music and want to pick up any tips I can.

What I found out shocked me.

The string "samples" he was using were not from any of the outstanding new sample libraries.

He was using virtual instrument software that was over *ten years old*.

Tell Me Why

I listened to his song again, studying the orchestra. It was amazing. Every note, every phrase, every nuance had purpose, meaning and was played with intention and feeling.

I realized the flaw I have been noticing in my own work lately. While it is important to have orchestra samples that sound pretty good it is even more important to write *great* arrangements and play each string part like a string player would.

Great samples are not a substitute for great arrangements.

Why do I tell you this? Because I think in this day and age of truly fabulous sounding sample libraries it is easy for us to bring up a wonderful string section, play some notes, and simply exclaim, "that sounds cool – I'm a friggin' genius!" And we do this before we have even begun to scratch the surface of creating a perfect arrangement.

It is easy to fall in love with an uninspired arrangement simply because today's orchestra samples sound so good and not because we have written an outstanding arrangement or played each part with emotion.

Go Back

It would probably be a great exercise for every orchestra sample library user to go back and get an average, old piece of virtual instrument software and learn how to make its orchestra sound amazing. We would need to dig deep into the parts we were writing, paying close attention to how each instrument was articulated as we would no longer be able to simply rely on fabulous sounding samples to carry our productions.

I have been producing some Frank Sinatra type songs these last few months and have been doing a lot of listening to the big band and orchestra arrangements of his old hits. One thing that struck me right away while studying these old hits is that nothing in any arrangement is a "throw away" line.

Each violin and viola, every trombone and flute, the saxes and the trumpets – everything – has purpose and is played with intention and expression. Nothing at all sounds like it was played by some guy hitting a few keyboard chords and triggering a virtual instrument library.

One good way to approach the arrangement and performance using a virtual instrument orchestra is to actually play each violin part – one note at a time. Then do the same with all of the instruments refraining from ever playing a chord on the keyboard. It takes a bit longer to do it this way but can add a great deal of realism to your arrangement.

For Me

I guess I am writing this as much for me as I am to encourage you. I need to remind myself (especially with my new sample libraries) that just having great sounds is not enough.

In addition to having great sounds, what truly makes a composition *sing* is writing a great arrangement, composing a great song and getting a great performance on each and every instrument. And then capturing it all on tape – so to speak.

In other words – don't settle. Rewrite your parts until they mean something.

Dig deep.

Turning a demo into a Master

You are about to discover one of the biggest secrets in making a demo sound like a master recording.

It is not about the software you purchase or sitting in a million dollar mastering facility.

It has little to do with compression or limiting and nothing to do with what DAW you are using. Nor does it have anything to do with any FX or some type of abracadabra thing.

Most recording engineers won't admit to it and yet virtually every multi-hit record producer will swear by it.

What is "it?" Wait - are you ready?

It's called "the vocal." It is about having the right vocalist - the *perfect* vocalist on any given song.

First Things First

Let's assume everything about your recording is pretty darn good. It needs to be - that is a given. You must have a good song and arrangement. Your players must have laid down tight tracks, the music must groove and be "in the pocket" so to speak. Your instruments and sounds must be recorded cleanly and mixed or balanced in a professional and solid way.

Assuming you have achieved all of these necessities at some point in your process you will have asked a vocalist to lay down the vocal track. Maybe you'll take a few passes. Maybe you will record multiple vocal tracks. Maybe you are the type to mix and match, "comping" (compiling) a part to get as near to perfection as possible. The vocal you have recorded is good - darn good. Your EQs and FX are as best they can be. You finally mix the song. You then listen back. It sounds good - in fact it sounds real good - but it still sounds like a demo. Albeit a quality demo.

But why?

Why doesn't it sound like a Master - like a finished record?

I'll tell you. *It is because you have the wrong vocalist singing the song.*

"But my vocalist is great," you say, "one of the best singers in the city!"

It doesn't matter where the singer came from or who they are related to if your song still sounds like a demo.

Listen to this next phrase and try to understand its meaning: "Even the great Pavarotti won't sound 'good' singing in the style of a George Strait song."

I have sat down time and time again with other producers listening to songs we have recorded using *real good* vocalists - sometimes even a studio pro vocalist - and the songs at best sound like very good demos. We have then listened to some of those *same songs* where the only thing that was changed in the entire recording was the actual *vocalist*. Amazingly, with the new vocalist those very same songs sound like *freaking killer Masters.*

Why? Because we found the *right* vocalist - the *perfect* vocalist for any particular song.
A lot of musician types will disagree with me. But between you and me, they are wrong.

I cannot emphasize this enough. The perfect vocalist can turn a good demo into a master recording.

But I Can Sing

I am a singer. I have made much of my living as a vocalist. My vocal has even been on hundreds of radio stations, TV shows and jingles yet *most* of the time these days I do not sing on my own recordings. Why?

There are two main reasons for this. One is that I simply cannot be objective about my own vocal performance. The other more important reason is the fact that my vocal is not the *right* vocal for most of the songs I write and produce. Yes, my vocal works well on a few styles but on most styles it does not make the song sparkle. If I use my voice on those recordings they will sound like demos - never masters.

Believe me when I tell you this; *the vocal is what sells the song.* (I can audibly hear hundreds of guitar players crying out right now, exclaiming, "No, it's the guitar that sells the song, stupid!" Again, they are wrong.)

It - *the lead vocal* - is your pitchman, you marketer and your best advocate. It is your image and the branding of your product. If the vocal is not the perfect fit you will probably not be able to sell your song. At least not in this day and age. I wish it wasn't so - but it is.

"But I can sing anything," some vocalists will proclaim. To them I would counsel, "Maybe you can, but your voice is not the *perfect* voice for everything."

My voice will work quite well on a Nat King Cole style song but it will suck a bag of pickles if I try to make it sound like

Soundgarden, or Wilson Pickett, or Rufus Wainwright.

Please note that if you are a recording artist-vocalist I am not talking to you here. You are what you are. Just be authentic and compelling in everything you do and write or find songs that *fit your voice*.

It is the rest of you producer-songwriter types I am speaking to. If you are recording blue-eyed soul you need to have a vocalist that *kills* in that style to make your song shine. If you are recording and producing in the Soundgarden vein you better have a vocalist that rivals Chris Cornell.

Yes, they are out there, these perfect-for-your-song vocalists. Do not, however, use that brilliant Chris Cornell style singer you have found on your Country tracks. They will probably stink and will not sound authentic at all.

Where Are They?

So, where do you find this great vocalist? Anywhere and everywhere. Today we have this wonderful thing called Google where you can actually search for the vocalist who might fit your particular style of music. Most serious, professional vocalists will have samples of their work that you can listen to on the web.

Be a bit cautious when it comes to the possibility of hiring the great singer from that band you saw playing last Friday night down at your local club.

They may have rocked the stage but there is a big difference between being compelling in a live venue and being the perfect voice on tape. It is doubtful that Sally Sugarmeister from the band down at the local watering hole will get the same results as a studio pro. Sally will probably sound good enough but your song will most likely sound like a demo and sit on your studio's shelf forever.

Having said that, I have had some good luck with a couple of local singers in the past who I used for specific songs – so you never know. Just be cautious.

Oh, and by the way, in case you haven't yet heard - no one produces demos anymore. Work-tapes, yes. But with all of the potential uses for music these days, with digital recording and with great samples, you need to be of the mindset that you are always producing masters. With Film and TV cues, Video Games, Advertising, Corporate Video soundtracks and Ringtones to name a few, there are numerous avenues for your mastered music to generate income even if it never becomes a hit.

In conclusion

There are many things that go into making a great record - into making a *master recording.* But if you have done all of those things and your song still sounds like a demo, take a long hard look at the vocal and try recording a few new vocalists on it. Find those people who are a perfect match for the genre and feel of your production. You will be surprised. Well, that's the secret no one will tell you. And now you know.

Cataloging Music Samples (Saving Time)

Eeek!

I can't find it. I know it is in here somewhere. Somewhere in my Omnisphere (Virtual Instrument) software that is. I know it is here because I remember hearing it. I remember playing it. But where the *heck* is it? (sigh) OK, I'll just listen to each sound - one by one – there's only a few thousand to get through - until I eventually find it again.

Thousands

I don't know how many of you have used the Spectrasonics VI called Omnisphere. If you haven't, give it a try. It is pretty cool. Omnisphere has some great sound presets that you can manipulate quite easily. Actually, it has *thousands* of great sounds - and that was my problem.

You see, I was producing a dance/club track and I remembered hearing this cool sound in Omnisphere months ago but I had neglected to write down its name. So I was stuck doing a sound by sound search for it.

Two hours later I finally found it and just as I had hoped with just a minor few tweaks it was the perfect fit for my club track. The problem was I had just wasted two hours looking for something I could have found in two minutes if I had only categorized and labeled it.

Granted two hours is not a lot of time to lose - but what if you *never* cataloged the cool sounds you found? Think about it. If you go on a prolonged search for a particular *lost* sound a few dozen times every year you could be losing as many as 100 hours of valuable recording time each year.

100 hours of lost recording time each year may not matter much to the person who is producing full time (I'll bet it does) but many producers have full time jobs *outside* of the music world and must produce their tracks in those precious few hours in the evenings and on their days off.

In fact, I know quite a few really good producers and composers who, because of their day gigs and family life, only get about fifteen hours each week to create music. To them, 100 wasted hours every year is a large percentage of their available and valuable time.

Cool Sounds

A few years ago, after becoming frustrated with wasting so much of my time doing sound-sample searches I started to catalog all of the cool sounds I found on each of my virtual instruments. I wanted to be able to easily access those little used but unique pieces of ear candy I had discovered.

It should be noted that when I first set up a new piece of software like Omnisphere I will spend many hours listening to and discovering the many cool preset sounds it has to offer. This is necessary time spent. I will usually start cataloging some of the unusual sounds I think I may use right there and then. For me there is no real need to log the sounds I use frequently because repetition will cause me to remember where they are located.

For example, in Omnisphiere I know exactly where some of the traditional sounds like Acoustic Guitars and Bells are and I have my *go to* patches etched into my skull simply from using them again and again. But those other sounds - the ones that are uniquely cool but rarely used - need to be cataloged somewhere for quick access.

As I said, I usually catalog those cool sound discoveries when I am first using a new piece of recording software. Unfortunately, I neglected to do that with the dance-club sound I told you about earlier. Eventually I found it and it worked perfectly. And I have now cataloged it for future reference.

Catalog

So how do I catalog the cool sounds I find?

It is really simple. I have created a file labeled "Cool sounds." (Original, huh?) Inside of the file are documents each with the title of a particular piece of software. (I.e. "Omnisphere.") In that document I have written categories for various styles of music or production usages such as Metal, Orchestra, Retro, Dance, Pads, Textures, etc. Under these category labels I then list the name of the cool sound I have found, often with a brief description and the software *path* in which to find it.

The category for the *cool dance-club sound* that I originally forgot to log now looks something like this:

Omnisphere
    * Style: Dance/Club/Fashion
    * Name: "Metropolitan Minimalism" (urban, club, chill)
    * Path: ARP + Rhythm > Metropolitan Minimalism

And that's it.

Another example of a preset sound that I might like to use is:

Omnisphere
    * Style: Pads/Textures (glue, warm fillings, not too harsh)
    * Name: "Pop Combo Male + Female Ahs"
    * Path: Human Voices > Pop Stacks > Pop Co Male + F. Ahs

If you are familiar with Omnisphere these above "paths" will make perfect sense to you. If you are not familiar with Omnisphere it doesn't matter. You can log your own path sequence *any way you want* with each of your own virtual instruments. As long as the path makes sense to you and helps you to instantly find your desired sounds – it is a good path.

Boring?

I know cataloging can sometimes seem like a boring and tedious thing to do unless organization is your favorite pastime. In that case, if you are a master organizer (and I do know a few) you have probably already cataloged all of your stuff and I'm not telling you anything you don't already know.

But for the rest of us, as boring and tedious as it may seem, it only takes a couple minutes of cataloging to save a couple hours or more down the road.

So there you have it. Yet one more trick to make you even more productive and efficient than you already are.

Now go bore yourself.

Anatomy of a Redneck Track

Today I'm going to write and record a Redneck, Southern Rock track.

Why?

It's for a show called *Duck Dynasty* (A&E) which has been using a lot of my music lately.

I thought I'd jot down my process so you can compare it with yours.

Maybe we can both learn something.

Note: This is not the only process of working I use.

But it is my process today.

Time: 1:15 PM

I have just entered my studio and am now turning on all of my stuff and opening up my DAW. I'll cue up a couple of audio tracks and add an EQ plug-in just to be ready in case inspiration strikes quickly. I am also opening up a few midi tracks and loading an old piece of music software called Sampletank.

I'm using my Sampletank software because if I find a cool guitar-riff idea I may want to add some quick drums to play my riff to and I am really fast at getting drum sounds out of Sampletank. Sometimes it helps me to play better guitar when I have an actual drum beat rather than just a click track to be inspired by.

I have grabbed my Fender Strat off its stand and I'm running it through a POD - Line 6 and then into my board. (And then out of the board and into my DAW). My first order of business is to simply start playing around with Southern Rock type guitar licks and hope that lightning strikes.

3:15 PM

I have finally found a rockin' guitar riff and after laying down a kick drum (4 on the floor at 144bpm) I have recorded two tracks of the riff (on different amp settings for wider frequency response) so that I can pan the guitar both left and right.

Although I am hearing a Jerry Lee Lewis banging piano part in my head, I am going to put down a basic hi-hat and snare before I head over to the keys.

I have decided to stick with the kick I already have and add a Sampletank hi-hat. For the snare I've loaded EZDrummer's Nashville kit. I am also putting in some EZ/Nashville toms. It is starting to sound pretty rockin' so I think I might be on the right path.

The cue is only 1 minute and 6 seconds in length. If I need more length I'll just loop the whole thing (copy and paste) to 2:12.

I am going to try to crank this track out quickly so I am staying on Sampletank and adding its KW piano and P-Bass.

Bam. Done. Coolness. They both rock!

4:30 PM

This thing is groovin' right along and it feels pretty tight. (I wish you could hear it). I am now going to slam down a B-3 organ part as well as some crashes and then I'll listen and evaluate what ear candy I may need. (Right now this cue is just screaming for a "bar fight" TV scene, or "4-wheel truck racing through a muddy field" scene.)

After getting a solid B-3 part and putting the cymbal crashes in their proper places I am now listening to what I have and tweaking the mix. (Note: I am mixing as I go. This is not always my M.O. but I'm going for speed today.) My gut reaction upon first listen is that this song could use a blues harp (harmonica) at the intro and maybe a chugging blues harp throughout to help give it even more of a Southern Redneck attitude. I think it also may need a dirty lead guitar riff at the "B" section for color and lift.

5:30 PM

I am now recording the harmonica up close on a SM58 mic. It sounds good and dirty like a bar band harmonica. After adding the B section guitar riff I am ready to tweak the mix.

It sounds pretty cool to me. There are no real holes to fill and it draws you into the Southern Rockin' Redneck feel right from beat one. This is good. I'll now run the whole mix through Ozone 3's CD mastering setting – tweak it a bit - and then print off an mp3-192 file so that I can listen to it tomorrow on a couple of systems and see if I am *there*.

I think it's pretty much done.

6:00 PM

Yup - the cue is *in the can*. (Pending tomorrow's double check.)

I think I'll go make a sandwich.

Note: The writing and recording of this track went *very fast*. It took just a little under five hours to complete. There are several reasons for this. First of all, it was a very simple piece of music to construct. The whole composition was based around a guitar riff and a simple 1-4-5 chord progression.

The instrumentation, too, is simple. Bass, drums, guitars and keyboards with a harmonica added. In addition, I spent *zero* time searching for sounds. I knew exactly what drum, bass, keyboard and guitar samples I was going to use because I have recorded this style of music dozens of times before.

Lastly, the track was only 1:06 in length. Had I recorded a full 2 or 3 minute track I could have easily added a couple more hours to my recording time. On average I can usually record a track in a style I am familiar with in 4 to 6 hours. Some take 8 to 10. If I am writing a vocal song it can take weeks to find all of the best lyrics.

The important thing is not the amount of time it takes to record a song, the important thing is that it sounds really good when you are finished. This one sounded pretty greasy – just like a Rowdy Redneck Bar Band song should.

Collaboration

Truth be told, I probably shouldn't be writing a chapter about collaboration. Not that I don't collaborate - I do, and often. It's just that I am one of those people whose natural tendency is to try to *do-it-yourself*.

I don't know exactly why this is.

Maybe I have an over inflated ego and actually believe I can do it better by myself. Maybe it is because I am overly competitive - because I want to win the race against everyone including myself. I often seem to feel the need to prove to myself that I can indeed do it all.

Yet even with my high desire to do it all single handedly I find time and again I am collaborating with others - and enjoying it! And more often than not I *get a way better end result* through collaboration than I would have gotten if I had stayed with the do-it-yourself plan.

What Are Collaborations in Music?

Collaborations can be co-writes, co-productions, getting second opinions on mixes or tempos or even simply using other musicians. You can collaborate in online forums, via Skype, on a street corner or anywhere else. Collaborations can be whatever you want them to be with whomever you want them to be with. The only rule pertaining to any musical collaboration is it must involve someone other than just yourself.

Many of my collaborations have been absolutely imperative to my success. There are scores of cues I couldn't have placed without collaborators. As a wonderful side benefit I have developed many lifetime friendships working with people in this way.

The Couch

A couple of years ago my wife purchased an "L" shaped couch for our TV room. She was absolutely thrilled to have gotten this piece of furniture and was excited to test drive it in our house. This gigantic L couch was delivered to our house by a couple of generous movers. It was sitting in two large sections inside of our garage when I got my bright idea.

The day after it arrived my wife was gone and I thought there would be nothing cooler for me to do than to get this new couch set up and in place in our TV room before she got home – kind of a happy surprise for her.

I did all of the prep work. I deep cleaned the room where the new couch would sit. I prepared a couch-path from our garage, up two flights of stairs, past the kitchen and through the narrow doorway to our sunken TV room. I even laid down a few heavy blankets so I could slide each section of the "L" couch to its final destination.

I thought moving the couch would be a snap. I was wrong

The trouble began as soon as I started tugging and pushing the first section out of the garage toward the stairs. It was heavy – *really* heavy. I wasn't more than two minutes into my moving extravaganza when the front arm of the couch slid off of the guide blankets and onto the rough, concrete garage floor.

The force and momentum of my pushing action did not allow me to stop quickly. The couch's soft fabric slid a few inches against the coarse concrete surface and yes - I ripped the arm. A string of inappropriate words immediately flew out of my mouth following this incident. I was ticked off at myself but even more determined to get this stupid thing upstairs.

I didn't notice it at the time but all of the joy I had initially felt for serving my wife had completely evaporated and was now being replaced by anger and frustration.

I somehow managed to get the couch up the first level of stairs without further incident but when I began negotiating the corners of our kitchen and the narrow hallway I got stuck.

"I will not be defeated!"

"I will get this couch into the TV room and set up all by myself if it is *the last thing I ever do!*"

I'll spare you all of the gory details but it *was* the last thing I did for quite some time. That's because in trying to get it through the house using only my own strength – I blew out my back. I screwed up a disc. My do-it-yourself plan had really done me in.

My wife was not happy when she got home. Not so much because the couch wasn't in place or had been ripped but because I had been stupid and stubborn enough to injured myself.

It was really so simple. All I had to do was call one friend. One friend to come and help me for thirty minutes. I'll bet I could have even found someone to do it before my wife had come home that day. Then I could have experienced the fullness of the joy I had wanted to see in her that day. Instead I got to experience the searing pain of a disc pressing against a nerve in my back.

I strongly recommend collaboration in music – as well as couch lifting.

Collaboration: It is a good thing. And sometimes quite necessary to achieve your desired result.

Imperfections

I was recently watching an episode of the TV show "*The Bachelor*." (That's right – *The Bachelor*. Please don't revoke my man card.) I know it is probably lame of me to be watching some contrived show about magically finding a fairy tale romance but what can I say - it is my guilty pleasure.

On this particular date episode of *The Bachelor,* the actual bachelor and one of his dates were dining in an unbelievably picturesque and romantic location. I think it was Tahiti. Anyway, it was a spectacular postcard perfect South Pacific setting.

The producers of the show had set up a dinner table at the end of a dock extending out over the warm water and underneath a little grass hut. This makeshift tropical restaurant had no walls or windows. It simply opened up onto the gorgeous outdoor evening. The couple had candlelight, red wine, exotic looking food and were engaging in what I would call fairly awkward small talk.

It wasn't going too well. I was actually feeling a bit uncomfortable for the both of them.

I mean here they are, perfectly dressed – he looked like he just stepped out of a GQ magazine ad, and she was elegantly attired in a soft, flowing evening gown - yet both of them appeared… well, clumsy.

Suddenly she says to him, "Was that a raindrop?" He replies, "I think it was." Within seconds they, in their little grass hut, are fully engulfed in a raging tropical rain storm. There was no escape. The wind gusts were insidious and the torrential downpour was hitting them sideways. For an instant is seemed as if their date was a total failure. Then something crazy happened.

He yelled to her, "We'd better make a run for it - back to the hotel." Then they both broke out in a very natural laughter, held on to their wine glasses, grabbed the bottle and darted off toward the hotel.

The very next scene has them drying off in his hotel room. She is now dressed in one of his oversized shirts and he in a much less GQ looking in a pair of blue jeans and T-shirt. Her fabulous hair style was gone. Killed by the rain. There is no more grass hut or exotic meal served on pristine waters under a symphony of starlight. Nope - they are just two regular people in a regular hotel room.

But now our bachelor and bachelorette are all cuddled up together laughing and giggling, engaging in some genuine, fun conversation. It is wonderful, authentic and truth be told - pretty romantic.

But why? Why did the perfect place – the restaurant hut on the water - seem so clumsy and how did something so failed become so beautiful?

Because they got *real*. Because it wasn't too contrived anymore. Because none of the perfect clothes or fancy hairstyles or South Pacific and candlelight really mattered. What mattered was honesty. Broken, flawed, genuine and wonderful honesty.

Music Production

It is so easy in this day and age of incredible music software to make a production sound perfect. You can use really cool sampled drums and bass. You can quantize them to be rhythmically flawless. You can add a Steinway sampled piano and a virtual instrument B3 organ. You can even find an amazingly sampled guitar and play the exact same guitar notes, articulations and chords into your keyboards that a guitar player would play. The options for great sounds perfectly placed in your production are limitless.

But sometimes when you record all that stuff and then listen back to your sonically perfect groove.... it stinks. It falls flat. It lies dead in the water. Even with your twenty-thousand dollars' worth of software your music sounds like a stiff, lifeless machine.

Tom Petty once said that he would never use a drum machine because his heart did not beat in perfect rhythm. While I won't go quite as far as he did I do concur with his sentiment.

At the end of the day our music needs to sound human (unless it is electronic music) and if it is too perfect, it will not breathe like a human breathes. Humans are flawed. Wonderfully flawed. And it is those very flaws that people have, those imperfections in human nature, we so often find the most interesting.

Just like our bachelor and bachelorette on their "perfectly" boring date, it wasn't until the night became flawed that they were able to enjoy being real.

Whether it is a bass note not completely locked in with the kick, or oboe notes that are not all evenly written into your recording software - whether it is the bending of a guitar note or the fact that a string player cannot bow in one direction indefinitely - a music production with slight imperfections will sound much better than one programmed to perfection.

There is an old saying that goes something like this, "light can only shine through a cracked pot."

Let your pot be a little... cracked.

Takeaways (Chapters 15 – 20)

1. Don't simply rely on the latest greatest virtual instruments to make your song sound good – write a great arrangement.

2. Try playing each virtual orchestra instrument separately (instead of chording them on a keyboard). This will lead to a more realistic sound.

3. Listen to and study real orchestras. They will teach you both arrangement and articulation.

4. Articulate each and every virtual instrument as a real player would.

5. A good singer will make your song sound like a good demo.

6. Finding the *perfect* vocalist for any given song can turn a demo into a master.

7. If you want to save enormous amounts of time in the long run catalog the sound names of your virtual instruments.

8. Learning and cataloging all of your instruments and recording gear will make you faster and more efficient in the studio.

9. Collaboration is often necessary to achieve desired results.

10. Collaboration can lead to unexpected and pleasant surprises.

11. Don't over-perfect your productions. They need to sound human and humans aren't perfect.

CaffeeVanillaCaramelMochaMacchiatoConPannaCinnamonStrawberryGreenTeaChaiBean Frappuccino

What would happen if you walked into Starbucks and ordered a Caffe Vanilla Caramel Mocha Macchiato Con Panna Cinnamon Strawberry Green Tea Chai Bean Frappucinno - and they actually gave it to you?

Let's think about it another way. What would happen if you took all of your favorite food flavors down to a Starbucks and had them mix them all together into one delightful drink? Would you like the way it tasted?

Probably not. It would most likely taste horrible and you would spit it out.

Another question.

Why do you think it would taste so awful? Yup, exactly! There would be *way* too many conflicting flavors all competing for your taste buds' acceptance.

Let's set of a different type of scenario with another question.

Have you ever been in a room or at a dinner table where everyone is trying to talk at the same time? What happens when everyone is loudly jabbering all at once? Even though a lot is being said, you really aren't *hearing* much of anything are you? With everyone talking at once it's just a bunch of noise.

Recording

Recording, producing and mixing music responds in much the same way. Each and every part you record needs room to breathe, a place and a space to be heard. It doesn't matter how cool the guitar part is, if it is competing for attention with the lead vocal and the keyboards, it won't be heard. Neither will those other parts. It will just be a jumble of mush.

In a conversation around the dinner table there needs to be a little give and take for it to be a real conversation. There needs to be a time when one person is talking and the others are listening. Then when someone interjects a word or a thought the lead talker will pause and give them their say before continuing.

At some point the conversation may even be passed off to a new lead talker but if it is a healthy conversation there is always a give and take, a back and forth.

In life there needs to be spaces, pauses, a *call and response* if you will, for a real conversation to take place. You cannot have true communication with a bunch of busy talkers all competing for attention.

The same holds true in a musical conversation. A bunch of busy instruments should not all be playing at the same time and competing with one another for attention. In a phrase – they should all be *supporting* one another.

If the lead vocalist is singing, for example, the other instruments need to play their own specific support role. And if at the bridge section of a song the electric guitar is taking a riff then the other instruments need to take a supporting role highlighting the electric guitar's riffage.

Ingredients

Although you and I may enjoy many different Starbucks drinks it is highly doubtful that any of us would enjoy those drinks if they were all mixed together. The ingredients that make a successfully delicious drink need to be complimentary to one another and mixed together in just the right amounts to satisfy our taste buds.

And so it is with music production. The drums, bass, electric guitars, keyboards, vocals and any other instruments must be carefully measured and mixed together, each complimenting one another in such a way that the listener hears the *song* - not one individual instrument taking over. *The song needs to be the star*. The same principle holds true for any effects, compressions or EQs. They, too, need to have a supporting role in helping to make the *song* the *star*.

Note: Even before you get to the production part of recording you need to be sure that the song itself was written with this same *perfect measurement* of love and care.

It should also be noted that when you or I are drinking our Starbucks concoctions what we *don't* usually think is "oh, that was the perfect amount of caramel" or, "what a splendid measurement of hazelnut my barista put in this cup today." Rather, we most likely just want to sip on our beverage and have it taste perfect.

Review

So, with all that said, let us review a few song production points:

1. Don't let everyone talk at once.

2. Get the perfect measurements of your song's ingredients.

3. Make sure all your ingredients are complimentary to one another.

4. Remember "the song is the star."

5. Be certain that you do all of the above in your song before you start recording.

Now let's go get some coffee.

Clutter

...not to belabor the point – but allow me to belabor the point.

"Simplicity is the ultimate sophistication."- Leonardo Da Vinci

In the house where I currently live there is a two-car garage. Actually, it's a little bit bigger than a two-car garage because it is quite deep. You can easily fit two large cars side by side in this garage and if you could make a car's four wheels turn sideways you could squeeze in a third car too.

The odd thing about my big garage is that my cars are seldom parked there. They are all parked outside in the driveway in every kind of weather. Whether it is hot, raining, hailing, freezing or snowing my cars sit exposed.

I have always dreamed of having a cool workshop area in my garage. Over the years I have been collecting tools of all sorts. I even built a work bench and have a bunch of shelves along one side of my immense garage.

However, I don't do any work with these tools in my garage.

Houses and junk

Some years ago my wife and I bought the house we currently live in. It is the same house with the big garage I was just telling you about. This house seemed really big to us when we first bought it. It may be small by some people's standards but we thought it was big. The mortgage was big, the taxes and monthly payments are big – therefore we call it a big house. Sometimes, when money is tight I call it a big-ass house. And sometimes, when we can't even afford to go on a vacation down to the local Motel 6, I have cursed our big-ass house.

Funny thing about houses – when you get one you look around at all of the empty space and start imagining all the stuff you want to buy to fill up this empty space. First there are chairs and couches, then a dining room table and a kitchen table. Some years you make a little extra money and you replace the old tube TV with a gigantic flat screen. Then you discard your old double bed for a new queen or king size bed.

Next thing you do is you have a few kids. Amazingly, these little children all seem to come with *their own stuff*. All you have to do is announce that you are having a child and a bunch of people start bringing cribs and strollers and electric swings and highchairs to you house – and then they leave. But all the stuff they brought to your house stays.

Pretty soon your kids demand that you get a cat and a dog to come and live in your house. And both the cat and dog have their own stuff. They have scratching posts to climb on and crates to sleep in and you need to build a couple of extra drawers to put leashes and rubber bones and a stuffed toy mouse in.

Another phenomenon about kids and pets is there are times when they need to go to the doctor, dentist or veterinarian. All of those places will send you a bunch of paperwork – a bunch of bills. You need to store that paperwork next to boxes of envelopes. Why? Because after you have carefully looked at the paperwork you will write and send huge sums of money in these envelopes back to the doctors.

And then the money you are paying the doctors causes you to want to have insurance and the insurance companies, in turn, will want to send you more papers and booklets and you will find yourself building a cupboard just to store all of that additional insurance paperwork in.

It is a vicious cycle of collecting junk with a snowballing effect.

Then

This goes on year after year and one day your wife decides it would be fun to start going to garage sales every week. So every Saturday morning you go treasure hunting and buy a whole bunch of junk that you thought was really cool while you were looking at it in someone else's garage at 9AM on a Saturday morning.

Pretty soon your house is not only filled with all of your necessities, it is overflowing with all your cool new junk. The stuff you bought from garage sales. You decide that you can't keep it all in your rooms so you start putting the "not-so-used" stuff in your garage. At first it is neat and organized but soon it gets cluttered. So you build shelves on every wall and then you build hanging shelves from the garage ceiling and before you know it all of the storage space is filled up and you are back to creating more clutter.

At first, one of your cars will still fit into the garage but after a few years of collecting all the stuff you thought you couldn't live without no cars will fit in your garage anymore.

It messes with your mind

If you are like my wife this doesn't bother you too much but if you are like me the clutter starts to bug you. It starts to feel like it's taking on an evil life all its own. You think about it at night. You imagine just throwing all that stuff on the street letting the rain wash it away. You even start blaming your wife, saying it is all of *her* stuff and all you really want out of life is about four feet of space in your garage so that you can hammer a nail into a piece of wood. You don't really want to build anything, you just think that it would feel nice to hammer a nail into a piece of wood.

Your frustration turns into a couple of arguments. You don't want to say mean things to your wife but you are feeling so frustrated by not being able to hammer a nail in your garage that it starts messing with your mind - like steroids or something. The final straw is when some neighborhood mice decide to take up residence in your jammed, crammed dump of a garage.

Genius

Out of desperation sometimes arises genius.

"Why don't we have a garage sale, clean this stuff out and only keep what we truly think we will use," you say to your agreeing wife, "and if anything is left over after the sale we will give it away or pack it up and truck it down to the local waste management station."

A deal is struck, a time is set. Sorting is done and decisions about all your stuff are made. People you don't even know come to your house, stand in your driveway and pay you money for all of your junk so they can take it home and look at it for a while and then put it in their garage with all of **their** other junk.

I'm okay with this because I know that one day they will become frustrated and they will have their own sale. I like to think of it as another variation on "the circle of life" or "what goes around comes around."

Well, we had our big sale – a couple of them actually. Then we trucked the left over stuff away and did a deep clean in our garage.

I can now park both vehicles in our garage and I also have a place to build stuff. My wife likes the organized storage spaces and quite honestly – as disgusting as our garage used to be – I would be pleased to show off this tidy new garage to anyone.

Less is more

You have already heard me say in this book that less is more. Right now I am going to say it again – *less is more*. We feel it in our hearts and minds and we know it to be true. If we try to cram too many activities and work into our week or if we get too many thoughts rolling round and round in our head, life just doesn't seem to work so well.

We need to simplify. We need to have some work, some play, some people time and some quiet, down time. When we simplify and balance things we are much less stressed, depressed, anxious and frustrated. That's just the way life works.

This same *less is more* principle holds true for recording and writing music. Sometimes we need to step back and take a good look at our songs. When we do this we will often realize that we have too much stuff in them. They are cluttered with all kinds of junk we once thought was cool. We have too many notes, lyrics, instruments and/or effects.

Our songs have no balance.

If, however, we clean out some of the stuff, take away some of the junk – if we simplify – our songs and our productions, like our lives and like my garage will become awesome showcases. Their "less" will become a lot.... more.

Ask yourself, "Do I really need this third guitar part?" Or, "Does the keyboard player really need to be playing eight notes all at once? Maybe two notes will do." And, "Does the verse really need twelve lines of lyrics? What would happen if I cut out four of those lines?"

Go ahead and question all of the potential clutter. "Does the drummer need to be playing a big fill through the last measure of every eighth bar?" "Should the singer be riffing over the drum fill?"

In our music, as in our life, it behooves us to remember that...

Less is more – more or less.

Spoons

A friend of mine who is a marriage counselor once told me about working with couples whose main issue is they have not learned how to argue correctly.

He says one of the major problems with many couples is they stop *listening* to each other. When they talk, they both talk over each other's sentences trying to force feed their opinions upon one another. Soon their one sided discussion becomes a heated argument because neither is feeling validated or respected by the other due to the simple fact that both are *talking* and neither is *listening*.

What my counselor friend suggests to these types of couples is that they practice an exercise in listening he calls "the spoon." What the couple is to do is to take a spoon – that's right, a kitchen spoon - and put it on the coffee table in their living room. (Note: never use a knife for this exercise.) Then they are to sit down and have a conversation.

My counselor friend goes on to explain, "When one person wants to talk, they need to pick up the spoon and hold it while they are talking. The other person is not allowed to speak as long as they do not have the spoon in their hand. When the first person (the one holding the spoon) is done talking they are to put the spoon back on the coffee table. Their partner can then pick up the spoon and as long as they hold it they will be the only one allowed to speak."

He goes on. "They are then to continue with their conversation in this manner, taking turns and using the spoon as a referee of sorts."

Brilliant!

While this exercise is no guarantee that each will listen to the other it does at least create an environment, a *space,* where listening is a possibility and where neither will be disrespecting the other with constant interruptions.

Conversation

As I've stated before, I think good music is a conversation. It's a conversation between the song and the listener. It is a conversation between each of the instruments playing. And if the song has lyrics it may even be a conversation between characters in the song's storyline and their emotional interplay with the person listening.

So many times when I critique the music of new writers, artists and producers I run up against the same thing. There are just too many notes. Their songs are too busy. Everyone is talking and no one is listening. (I've got tons of old productions of my own stuff that also are filled to the brim with too much noise)

My advice in these critiques is almost always the same. There needs to be a space where someone (some instrument) gets to hold the "spoon" while the other instruments, lyrics or melodies sit in support and *listen*. Sometimes the singer needs to hold the spoon and sometimes they need to put it down so the guitar player or drummer can hold it for a moment. The listener, too, needs to be afforded time to hold the spoon. To be able to interject his or her own emotion into the *receiving* and *interacting* experience of the song.

I also sometimes hear productions where there is so much constant chatter between instruments, FX and arrangement that the only emotion the song truly evokes is one of *tiredness*. These music productions are so chatty they suck the life out of the listener and *the listener stops listening*.

One of the things we as writers, arrangers and producers always need to ask ourselves in our musical conversations is, *"are we talking too much?"*

Fido Nashville (Less is More Unless More is More)

I'm sitting this morning in a little neo-hipster sidewalk coffee shop in Nashville, Tennessee called Fido.

I have parked my laptop at one of those window bars that looks out upon the foot traffic strolling across a red brick sidewalk underneath a perfect blue sky day.

The simple stout mug that rests on a deep wooden bar next to my computer holds my caffeine fix. It is called "Cafe Del Sol."

I chose the medium brew this morning and its flavor soothes my soul as much as its smooth taste brings a warm, comforting smile to my senses.

The pastry display case just behind me holds such an immense array of culinary temptresses that it has taken all of my willpower to resist them.

Patrons

The room is about half full. There are tourists with their "Nashville" T-shirts sitting in a few booths.

At the table behind me a couple of well-dressed middle aged gentlemen are talking in business terms about various country artists and the current state of the music industry as it pertains to marketing.

I guess them to be management types. They seem important. And they have an air about them that speaks the subtle message, "we want you to look at us and know that we are very important and quite powerful."

A contemporary hippie sits a few stools away from me. He looks to be twentyish. He has a bohemian look with his thrift-shop, carefully-mismatched clothes. His sandals and full head of perfectly muffed hair let me know he comes from money.

He also has a brand new iPad and iPhone. Maybe he is a student at nearby Vanderbilt or maybe he is in a band. He has the look of an understated indie-rock guy.

I think he is writing lyrics to a song as I type this. He probably wonders if I am some sort of a chill A&R executive in my casual blue jeans and Adidas sweat jacket. Maybe he is just another guy trying to make it through Chemistry class. I don't know.

June

It is mid June. There is a tree that rises out of the brick sidewalk up toward the smiling skies. It has hundreds of tiny leave sprouts on each of its limbs. It somehow reminds me that new life always finds a way.

The clientele here is truly eclectic. There are quite a few college dorm girls casually dressed, all playing with their hair while texting on their smart phones.

There are a couple of sports-type jock dudes just to the left of me. I don't want to look at them too long. I think they might beat me up. I also see a few aging cowboy types who could pass for Willie Nelson's brothers. I wonder if these old cowboys have had a hit song sometime in the past. It is Nashville, after all. There are thousands of songwriters in this town. Maybe they are the ones who came here long ago in hopes of being discovered and never found their dream but are still, even at the age of seventy-something, trying.

Conversation

The conversation echoes loud in this place. I like it. It is comforting and makes me feel as if I am part of something - as if I belong to this café family even though I am sitting alone. There is muffled music playing. I can't make out the artist. I wonder if it because of the elevated noise of the patrons or just bad speakers.

The walls in this place are made of brick - something that resembles cheap stucco. They are filled with what I presume to be works of art from local artists.

I just took a walk around the room and some of these oil paintings are actually quite good. When I was leaning over one particular table to get a better look I almost spilled my coffee of some young starlet who looks as if she is trying to be the next Taylor Swift. Maybe she will be. I should probably get her autograph now.

Yes, this is Fido on some anonymous morning in the West End district of Nashville, Tennessee. Can you feel it? Can you hear the cappuccino machine? Do you smell the fresh ground coffee beans and the steaming dishes as they come out of the kitchen? I hope so. I hope I have given you a little snapshot of my morning here in TwangTown.

Word, notes and rhythms

If you are getting any sense of this Fido place from my words, then ask yourself this question – Why? What would have happened if instead of using all of my overly descriptive language I would have simply said, "I am drinking coffee in Nashville." Would you have experienced anything then?

Did I use too many words and phrases or just the right amount? This is a question as songwriters and music producers we need to continually ask.

And how about all of those descriptive musical notes and rhythms - have we found that perfect concoction in our composition that will transport the listener to some special place, evoking certain emotions from him or her?

It's hard, isn't it?

Sometimes less is more. Sometimes more is more.

As artists we must discern the right mix of words, lyrics, paint, musical notes and everything else that goes into our creation. This is our job. We need to get the vision out of our minds and onto paper and then begin the hard work of crafting that vision into perfection.

It ain't easy.

I once read that a visual artist succeeds if you can *hear the music playing in his paintings.*

So, too, a music artist succeeds when they *paint pictures with their songs.*

Yes, many times the experience is in the details. But how many details? Quite often less is more. But sometimes more is more. You get to decide. Hang in there.

It will come.

Ricky & Lucy and the Ten Foot Bow

Have you ever watched reruns of the 1950s TV show *"I Love Lucy?"*

Do you recall the sleeping arrangements of the married couple Ricky and Lucy?

They slept in separate beds.

Yup, that's right. The television show depicted them, a married couple in real life and on TV, as sleeping in separate beds.

That was pretty much the norm of what was acceptable on TV in those days.

My-oh-my how things have changed.

Modern TV

It is pretty amazing to think that what was once considered the norm on TV was to see a married couple sleeping in separate beds.

It is also pretty astonishing to see what the TV norm has evolved to. Today when you flip through channels and watch reality shows, dramas, soaps, sit-coms and the rest, you will see married couples (and unmarried couples) sleeping pretty much anywhere and with anyone.

And they probably won't be wearing old fashioned pajamas and giving each other a simple smooch just before they turn out the lights. In modern day TV you see it all – or at least it is all implied. Almost anything goes.

That is the new norm. Anything goes is not very shocking anymore. It is fairly accepted by mainstream culture – at least in the USA – to see someone's explicit actions while bunking with multiple partners. But how did we get to the new norm from the old norm? How did we go from Ricky and Lucy in separate beds to anything goes?

I'm not sure how it happened. A little at a time I guess. However it has happened I think we can all concur that what is considered normal bedroom behavior on today's TV is a far cry from what was acceptable fifty years ago.

I am not commenting on whether this change is right or wrong or good or bad. I am simply noting that the norm has indeed shifted both on TV and in our minds.

Our Ears

In the last thirty years, due to technology, our musical ears have gone through some pretty significant changes as well.

Auto Tune and programs like it have caused us to be much more cognizant of pitch problems a vocalist may have. Listen to the vocals of songs from the 60s and 70s and you will hear pitch problems all the time.

Sure, the vocal performance on many of the hit songs back in the day was outstanding but if you listen to those songs now you will hear numerous intonation discrepancies. Why do we hear those discrepancies today when we didn't back then? I would like to submit that it is because our ears have been conditioned to a *new norm.*

What was once considered the norm in pop music – a great emotional performance – is no longer acceptable due at least in part to digital technology and to our ears being *conditioned* to hearing digitally corrected vocals.

There is a backlash to this phenomenon with many new bands and artists refusing to auto tune their vocals but as of right now I'd say our ears have been conditioned to a new normal when it comes to intonation.

Time

Another huge change in the last decades has been *time*. Due to the advent of digital drums, sequencers, click tracks and quantizing we rarely accept anything less than perfect or near perfect time from our popular musical performances.

After a few decades of perfectly sequenced drum tracks our ears are have become hyper aware if something isn't locked in time-wise. Even though a non-musician may not be able to articulate what is "wrong" with an out-of-tempo song he or she will sense that the performance isn't quite working.

If you don't believe me go back and watch the movie-documentary *Woodstock* and listen to how out of time many of those bands were.

The drummers in some of those groups are rushing the tempo so bad it is hard to listen to with today's ears.

Again, there is a backlash to this with some new bands refusing to use a click track in their recordings. So our ears might again change but by in large we are currently conditioned to think of near-perfect time as the acceptable norm.

Ten Foot Bow

All this reconditioning of our ears and the social engineering of what is the accepted norm for bedroom behavior on TV has got me thinking about the violin.

Yeah, the violin.

When I first started recording orchestrations (strings, brass etc...), not being a string player myself, I would quite often make the mistake of holding a violin part out (played, of course, on my keyboard) over four, five or even eight measures on the same note. It was pointed out to me that in order for a real violin player to play my violin part he or she would need to be holding a *ten foot long bow*.

For those of you who don't know, a violin player's bow is not nearly ten feet long.

I quickly learned that if I wanted to make my violins sound like the real deal I needed to play and articulate them as a real violin player would. If I was going to hold out one long note I needed to only hold it as long as a real violin player's bow could hold it.

If I wanted to hold that same note out a bit longer I would need to articulate it in the same way a violin player would while changing the direction of their bow. (You can clearly see that I am not an orchestra player because I don't even know the correct terminology for changing the direction of a bow.)

Doing this – getting rid of my ten foot bow - immediately made my strings sound more like a traditional orchestra.

And yet as I listened to and began studying pop music on the radio and production music in film and TV, I began hearing ten foot bows all over the place. This, I concluded, was due at least in part to uneducated composers (like me) playing their violin parts on keyboards without giving any thought to what a real orchestra player could or couldn't do.

Could it be that once again digital technology is changing what we play and the way we hear strings in much the same way it has done with how we hear vocal intonation and a drummer's time?

There are hundreds if not thousands of producers out there right now using a ten foot bow on their violin as they hold their finger down on the keyboard for eight measures. And they are saying "ooh, that sounds so cool!" And some of their music is making its way to our ears again and again.

So my question is: Over the next decade or two will our ears become so accustomed to hearing a *ten foot bow* that it will become completely acceptable and maybe even necessary to compose and perform our Pop orchestra music this new way – using a ten foot bow?

Will digital technology keep reconditioning our ears to new norms in music like the ten foot bow? Or will Ricky and Lucy continue to sleep in separate beds forever?

The bottom line for me is: *if it sounds cool, keep it.*

Takeaways (Chapters 22 – 25)

1. Less is more. Step back from your songs and see if *taking out* some elements might make them bigger and better.

2. Not every instrument or voice can speak at the same time. Leave space.

3. Identify which instrument(s) are speaking and which ones are listening and supporting the main voices.

4. Quite often lyrics can say a lot more with fewer words.

5. Sometimes more is more. Especially in Country songwriting

when you need to be more lyrically detailed. In certain genres more words and more descriptive lyrics may be required.

6. We must always strive to find the perfect balance between less and more pertaining to our lyrics, notes, rhythms and production.

7. Technology may be conditioning our ears to require better time and intonation in our songs.

8. The *new norm* may actually require our Pop song strings to use ten foot bows.

Light Bulbs - Film and TV Songwriting Lyrics

I wrote and recorded a really cool song a few years ago. At least, I thought it was pretty cool. I did a sparse, Corinne Bailey Rae type production on it and got a fabulous female vocalist to sing the lead.

The reason I think this song might have actually been pretty good is because although it never got cut by a major label artist it has been cut by a couple of indie artists. And back in 2008 it was a Top Ten most shared song on Facebook for a few days. I don't really know what that means but Facebook is fairly big so it probably means the song got quite a few listens.

Even though it wasn't a hit for me I thought this particular song, entitled "Better With You," sounded good enough to make me some dough with a few TV and movie placements. To my surprise the music supervisors and libraries I pitched it to were not as enthusiastic about my song as I was. In fact no one - NO ONE - in the film and TV biz who heard this song wanted it.

After a year or so of unsuccessfully pitching "Better With You" I decided this dog was just not going to hunt so I let it slip into the sad-face-file on my computer and accepted its inevitable fate.

But why - why did everyone pass on it? I mean, this thing sounded pretty darn good.

Revelation

A couple of months after casting this un-betrothed beauty into the depths of my PC's cellar I had one of those mornings where you go through your old forgotten songs in hopes of discovering a gem you might have missed. One by one you give those old throwaways another chance to become that diamond in the rough, hoping you will hear something in your old friends that might lead you in a direction toward finding it a new home.

I clicked play on my song "Better With You."

Suddenly the light bulb came on, the waters parted and I had one of those mountain top revelations. I was instantly and profoundly enlightened. I should have started a religion right there and then. I suddenly knew what was keeping this song from being considered as a foreground track in TV and film. Let me explain.

The first four lyrical lines of the song go like this:

A sunset on the beach
a small cafe
an old romantic movie
on a rainy day

Do you see it? It seems so clear to me now. Why did I not notice this before? Doh!
The first four lines of my song actual paint pictures of *four separate scenes.*

"A sunset on the beach." Well, we know what that is. It is a sunset – on a beach.

How about the second line, "A small café?" Ha! Maybe there is a café on the beach mentioned in the first line but probably not. I think when most people hear the phrase "a small café" they are not seeing a café in the sand on a beach.

Let's move on.

What about the phrase "An old romantic movie?" I suppose you could watch an old romantic movie on some beach somewhere but a glowing sunset would probably make it difficult to view. You could also possibly watch an old romantic movie at *a small café* but small cafés are often noisy so all of the customers' loud talking might disrupt the romantic mood of the movie you and your honey are watching.

Do you see where I am going with this?

The last line "on a rainy day" works well with watching *an old romantic movie* or being at *a small café* but it visually contradicts gazing at *a sunset on the beach*. If you have sun and rain at the same time you probably need to add a rainbow.

Okay. Here is the lesson.

Imagine you are a film's music supervisor and you are casting a song for a scene with a young couple walking on the beach at sunset. Would you want the lyrics "an old romantic movie on a rainy day" as a part of the music that helps to elevate the mood of your beautiful sunset?

No, is the correct answer.

In the same way if your film's scene was of a young couple watching an old romantic movie on a rainy day in their cozy condo while they snuggled on the couch, would you want the lyrics to speak about "sunsets" and "cafes" in that scene? Probably not.

I was thrilled with my new realization. I finally "got it." I understood why this song or these types of lyric combinations wouldn't work as a foreground track in a movie or on a TV show. This one verse was depicting four separate scenes. And as a filmmaker you usually need the music to elevate the mood of one visual and one visual only!

This light bulb revelation has truly helped me to revision my craft as I write new lyrics for film and TV. I wrote it down. I etched it in stone and signed it in blood. Lesson # 378 for film and TV lyric writing: *Keep all the lyrics in any given song focused on supporting one scene.*

Options

Does this discovery, this enlightenment, mean that my song "Better With You" is a bad song? Absolutely not. As I said earlier, this song has been recorded a couple of times and may be recorded again. It is a radio song, a song for artists to perform.

But, as far as TV goes, it is not a front runner for foreground music. It could be used in the background of a TV show as *source music* (one of the definitions of source music is music you hear playing *way* in the background when the characters walk into a restaurant or a bar while dialog is being spoken). In source music you don't always really *hear* the lyrics of those songs, you just *feel* that there is music in the scene. But source music is about the only use for it in Film and TV.

I could, however, rewrite the lyrics and keep them all in the same "scene" so to speak. Consider the above lyric. It could be rewritten like this:

A sunset on the beach
walking in the sand
it feels so good
holding your hand

Those may not be brilliant lyrics and I may not win a Grammy with them but they are all a part of *one beach scene.* They are also a bit less specific which always helps in Film and TV music. The downside to these lyrics is that the song would only be used for a beach scene so it is therefore somewhat limiting. However, on the plus side these new lyrics are better for a scene than the original lyrics.

If we wanted to go even more generic - less specific - we could make those first four lines say:

It feels so good
like a smile inside
when we're together
everything is right

Those lyrics may, indeed, suck, but they would work just fine in most any positive relationship scene. I think, however, I will throw them away, cast them aside and banish them into the "these lyrics will embarrass me" file.

Can you see how these last lyrics would be much more conducive to a scene for film and TV than my original lyrics were? Me too.

Ah. I love it when the light bulb finally comes on.

Songs for Sinatra (Writing Authentic Sounding Songs in Various Genres)

The last few months I have been writing songs for Frank Sinatra.

You heard me right - *Frank Sinatra.*

As you can imagine, writing songs for "The Chairman of the Board" presents at least a couple of challenges. First of all Mr. Sinatra is no longer with us. He passed away back in 1998. Secondly, even if he was still alive, I do not have the clout needed to get my songs to him.

Nevertheless, I am still writing songs and producing a Sinatra CD.

Style

I should probably clarify. I am writing songs in the *style* of the Frank Sinatra swingin' big bands and producing a CD of those songs for use in Film and TV. "Ah..." you say, "now I get it."

Important Note: Let me be crystal clear that one should never try to duplicate an artist's "voice" when using them as a reference nor should one ever use the melodies of an artist's song or arrangement. The singer's style may be emulated but not the singer himself (or herself.) Copying a signature voice such as Frank Sinatra or Tom Waits as well as copying song melodies can get you into legal trouble and is ethically misguided. When I use an artist such as Frank Sinatra for reference I am talking about capturing his vibe, attitude, the mood and the essence of the song's style as well as the vocal and instrumental phrasing of the era.

As I finished writing my first few songs for this project I immediately recognized a fairly substantial problem. Although I thought my songs were pretty good - they all sounded like standards - they didn't really sound like swingin' Sinatra songs. They sounded more like Nat King Cole, Mel Tormé and Bing Crosby than they did Frank.

The CD I am writing and producing is supposed to be in the stereotypical "Sinatra Rat Pack" style. It needs to have a very swingin' Las Vegas Strip sound to it. It needs to be hip, hep and *cool baby.*

Homework

Since my songs weren't sounding much like Frank's swinging "Rat Pack" I decided to do some homework. I needed to go back and not only listen to those Sinatra Vegas songs, I needed to study them. I needed to deconstruct them and find the perfect ammo with which to load my songwriting guns.

I cued up about twenty "Sinatra at the Sands" type tunes including "Fly Me to the Moon," "Luck Be a Lady," and "Come Fly With Me." Upon listening, one of the things I began to notice right way was I don't talk the way the Rat Pack did. I don't speak in their vernacular. I don't live the fast lane Vegas lifestyle. I don't call women "broads" and I don't often sit at the Craps table and "roll the dice." In fact, no one I know does any of these things on a regular basis.

This was going to be tough.

I reasoned that the best way to emulate the kind of lyrics Sinatra would sing would be to make a list of the most commonly used words and phrases in his songs. So the first thing I did was to scour his tunes and make a concise "words and phrases" list. I also jotted down the subject matter he would often talk about both in his songs and while on stage.

I listened to his music, his stage banter and his interviews and took notes. When I was done I had about one-hundred and fifty words and phrases including: Dice, Luck, Lady, Drinkin', Fly Away, Moon, Swingin' etc...

Once I had my list of Sinatra words I started to let them play in my imagination and began to formulate my own song phrases and story ideas. It was working. Some of my new stuff was beginning to sound like Frank would have done it.

As I mentioned above, I needed to be very careful not to copy any of the old Sinatra songs. I most definitely do not want to plagiarize anything, *ever*. It is always my intention when crafting music in a particular genre and using any specific artist's music as a template to make certain I am only emulating a particular style. To help me avoid being too close to his songs I took the approach that I was in fact writing new songs for Mr. Sinatra to consider recording. And if I felt at any time I was getting to similar to any particular song of his I stood by my old songwriting phrase: *When in doubt, throw it out.*

To be extra sure I was not crossing any legal lines I added to my template two more artists; Michael Bublé and Harry Connick, Jr. This gave me a broader spectrum of that big band swing style within which to work.

Music

The next thing I set out to do was to map-out the most common chord progressions to the biggest Sinatra hits from his swingin' Vegas style. I only wanted the hits. The biggest chart toppers. This is because they are the songs that have steeped themselves into our collective psyche. These hit songs are the ones that will trigger certain moods from the masses. It would make no sense to deconstruct an obscure Frank Sinatra song for the purpose of recreating a stereotypical mood for Film and TV. They would be less apt to evoke the needed emotion from an audience for a film's *Vegas type* scenes. Therefore, they would be less apt to get placed and make me any money.

I also checked out those same songs where I could with both Michael Bublé and Harry Connick Jr.

After I had charted out some commonly used chord progressions I went back to the Frank songs, listened again and steeped myself in Sinatra type melody. I just tried to soak it in and let it percolate. I listened to *a lot* of his music before I wrote. I started noticing trends in the way he would hold out certain vowels or snap short a certain word for emphasis.

You may think this kind of study would cause one to become bored and sick to death of an artist. However, the deeper I dug in, the more of a profound respect I had toward not only Mr. Sinatra's approach but for his songwriters and arrangers. They were truly some brilliant folks working with The Chairman back in the day.

Writing

Once I was thoroughly drenched in these sounds I took my lyric phrases, story ideas, chord maps and new melodic sensibility and revved up my creative engines.

In these writing sessions I would often start by cranking up a Frank Sinatra tune like "Fly Me to the Moon," then allow myself to get into the mood, tempo and feel of the song. After I had found the vibe I would quickly shut off the player's sound and jump over to my piano and let her rip.

At this point I was not editing myself at all. I was just looking for verses or choruses that *sounded like* Sinatra at the Sands. I would usually get an idea in just a few minutes, record it onto a cheesy hand held digital recorder and then move on to the next song.

I repeated this process for about two months with Sinatra, Bublé and Connick, Jr. At the end of that time period I had accumulated 46 song ideas in the big band style. I only needed twelve but I wanted to have an abundance of material to pick and choose from so that I could mix and match if need be. (I have found quite often that a verse for one song will work well with the chorus of a totally different song especially when I am working in the same song style.)

As I began to identify which were my favorite new song ideas I took on the job of finishing them. I tried to keep them as close to my target style as possible by referring back to the hits again and again. I wanted to stay true to the big band vibe and also make certain I wasn't copying or plagiarizing any of the music or lyrics.

Success - *just Swing, baby!*

I must say I am pretty pleased with my results. I now have twelve tunes all fitting very nicely with the Sinatra Rat Pack style. I have had to go back and edit out some of the specific lyric references in the songs to give them a broader TV and Film usage appeal. (If you use too many specific words in a song like the city "San Francisco" or the name "Guinevere" it severely limits potential uses in Film and TV.)

This particular songwriting process is one I have used with great success over the last few years. In fact, I just recently finished some Depeche Mode style instrumentals and some Swampy Slide guitar and harmonica instrumentals. Both of these styles of music were in genres unfamiliar to me so I needed to go and steep myself in both the Depeche Mode songs from back in the day and in some Swampy Blues songs. Again, as with the Sinatra type songs, I needed to actually deconstruct what the artists of those styles were doing so that I could recreate their vibes authentically.

Who knew that decades after college I would still have to do *homework*.

If a Picture Paints a Thousand Words (Visualizing)

Some of the best paying cues in TV, film, advertising and other new media are songs used as foreground music. A foreground song is music used when an actor's dialogue stops and you hear the music and lyrics as if you were listening to them on your home stereo system with the volume turned up.

These types of music placements are rare but they can be a great showcase for your material when you land one.

Sometimes the lyrics in these foreground songs need to be "generalized feelings" where the mood, instrumentation and vibe are of prime importance.

Other times, however, there is a spot in a scene for a more detailed lyric to shine. These types of TV song placements are indeed few and far between but I would like to take just a little time to speak to this style of writing.

Here we go.

Question...

Does a picture *really* paint a thousand words?

If so logic would suggest that all one needs to do to create song lyrics is to paint a picture in one's mind.

And then once that picture is perfectly *mind-painted* one should simply be able jot down all of the glorious phrases it speaks.

Right?

It can't be that simple can it?

Well, actually – it can be that simple. The trick is to learn how to *mentally* paint a perfect and vivid picture.

In other words, if we can exercise our Thalamus, which is buried somewhere in the Medulla, to better stimulate our Somatic Sensory Cortex – bingo – we're on our way toward creating a marvelous mental masterpiece.

Furniture

I am going to use the Country music genre as my canvas for this next section because country songs are known for their detailed and descriptive lyrics – more so than any other popular musical genre.

In country lyric writing there is a phrase you will hear thrown around a lot. That phrase is: "you've got to paint the furniture."

What this means generally speaking is country lyrics need to have more *details* than most other forms of popular music and those details need to be *real*.

The other popular music genres simply need to take the listener on an emotional ride. Sometimes this is achieved through lyrical story but quite often it is accomplished with melody, groove, vibe, a catchy chorus or any one of a number of other emotion stimulators.

Country music on the other hand will quite often have a very linear melody line (especially in the verses) relying heavily on pictures being painted through vividly detailed storytelling to trigger the listener's emotions.

One way to discover "furniture" lyrics for our songs is to *visualize* every nuance of the story we are trying to convey. In other words we need to *paint a picture of the story* in our mind before we attempt to tell it.

Visualize

I have never been good at remembering or memorizing text. I think this is why school was such a constant struggle for me. I could barely recall the correct answers needed to pass a test when I was studying by text. However, I could always perfectly answer test questions on anything I had learned *visually*.

For example, any and every day of my entire school career I could accurately describe in perfect detail any of my teacher's clothing. The colors, patterns and styles I can still recount to this day. I could also tell you what their hair styles and colors were and all of the accessories they might have been wearing down to their shoe laces.

In addition I could recount to you what each class member was wearing, all of the artwork and clippings on any wall, what the floors, ceilings and walls were made of as well as what shade the window blinds were and where the windowpane's painting was cracked or had been touched up.

I guess I am what they would call a *visual learner*.

Speaking

About fourteen years ago I started speaking in public. At first, this speaking in public thing terrified me. Why? Because I didn't want to look like an idiot in front of people.

I thought I would look like a fool because I would be stumbling over my words for the simple reason that *I can't memorize text*. It's true. I cannot for the life of me memorize even the simplest text, but I was about to discover something I *could* do.

I learned that if I could paint pictures in my mind of the stories I wanted to tell - if I could create little movie scenes in my brain - all I had to do while speaking in public was to play that movie in my mind, watch it as it unfolded and then narrate the scenes to my audience.

I have been using this trick for over ten years now and it works like a charm. I may indeed be stupid but at least I don't sound *too* stupid in front of a crowd. Usually.

Songs

Sometimes when I write lyrics for a song I will start by thinking of a title or a catchy phrase. In other words I start with text. This is really helpful as it gives me a "go" line or idea to focus on and some parameters to work within.

After establishing my song's direction with a title or a phrase it is important for me to next try and *visualize* the story. I need to *see* the characters. I need to watch what they are doing and sense how they are feeling. I need to paint the best pictures of their situation I can. Whether it be falling in love or falling out of love I need to brush color strokes upon the canvas in my mind and watch the characters as they act out their scenes.

I also need to see in detail what clothes they are wearing, the style of their hair, what age they are and where they live or where they are encountering one another. The more "furniture" I can put in their lives the better I can write.

If I can't see the characters clearly at first I will start asking myself questions about them such as:

Do they have a cup of coffee on a table in front of them?

Is that coffee warm or has it been sitting on the table for hours?

Is there an ashtray full of cigarette butts nearby - or not?

Is there a book of matches?

What is the logo on that book of matches?

Maybe there is a half empty bottle of Jack Daniels on the Formica next to the fridge or maybe one of the characters is holding lipstick in her hand while *looking at her life* in the mirror. Is she happy or sad? Is she empty or full? Who else is near her? What is the lighting in the room in which she stands? Is it dim or is it bright and painfully stark? Maybe it isn't a "her" holding lipstick - maybe it is a "him."

And on and on.

Let me give you one example of a lyric that has little furniture followed by the same lyric with an abundance of furniture.

She left me cold in the dark
I could barely breathe
My world was falling apart
I was drowning in grief

I know – not very original. Here's the same story with some furniture added:

I heard the door slam, her Pontiac engine roar
Took a half burned smoke and struck a light
With a bottle of Jack, on our old kitchen floor
I drank away her memory that night

Do you see the difference between furniture and no furniture?

The more vividly I can paint the picture or create the movie in my mind, the better I will be at communicating a story's emotions through lyric. Sometimes when the scene in my mind is utterly vivid the song seems to write itself.

Edit

Once I am done narrating the story playing in my mind I will need to go back and edit my lyrics, my lines and phrases making them all fit into a Country or Pop song format or into whatever genre I am writing in.

I will need to trim the fat and look for some words a little less cliché than what I have originally narrated. I will need to search and find fresher ways of saying certain things. But the story or emotional picture will be there ready for me to tweak.

If you are a person who learns very well from reading and imagining *text* – then, never mind.

But if you are a visual learner like me, give it a try.

Try painting a vivid, colorful and detailed movie scene in your mind *before* you put pen to paper or fingers to computer. Ask questions about each and every detail in these scenes. The *louder* or more vivid you can make your characters and furniture "speak" the easier it will be to translate their message to an audience.

So, does a picture really paint a thousand words?

Yes, I think it does and it can also help us write a few cool songs.

Step Away from the Song (Song REwriting)

Do you ever find yourself getting bogged down in writing a song?

Getting stuck. Knowing that you are onto something pretty good but all your potential paths to the finish line seem to be dead ends.

Do you ever spin your wheels for hours trying to find those last few perfect lyrics or that magic melody change?

I do.

Or, I should say, I *used to* run into that problem all the time.

Not anymore.

Catch and Release

Maybe the most useful songwriting skill I have learned and put into practice over the last years is the art of writing quickly *and then letting go.*

Let me explain.

When I have a song idea or when I have scheduled time to write music I usually work *very* quickly. I like to get as much of the song written as fast as I can. I usually spend no more than a couple of hours on the initial idea and then I let it go. What I mean by "letting it go" is when my brainstorming ideas come to an end I will record what I have and then put it away. I will not listen to what I have written for a minimum of two weeks.

I will resist the urge to bring it back out and start tinkering. This is because if I work on it too soon I will not be objective. I will either start messing with the wrong parts or I will falsely think I am a *genius* and then sit and listen to my *brilliance* over and over again. This will burn the song into my memory making future fresh and objective rewrites nearly impossible.

However, if I put the song away for a few weeks and in the meantime start working on other songs, when I go back to listen to it again it will sound completely fresh. I will have pretty much forgotten what I originally wrote and be able to listen to it with objective ears. Most always I will immediately know what needs to be fixed and changed to make the song really shine.

In this process I am acting as my own collaborator. It really does work quite well for me to approach my writing and rewriting in this way. I have recently discovered I am not the only one who thinks this process is a helpful and an important part of writing.

Six Weeks

Even the great author Stephen King says in his brilliant book *On Writing* that a writer should lay down their manuscript for a minimum of six weeks before giving it a re-read and a rewrite.

Listen to Mr. King. He knows what he is talking about.

Give It a Try

And so it is with songwriting and music composition. If we try to finish or correct our songs during our initial writing sessions we will need to do a right brain/left brain shift. We will move from creating to editing which are two entirely different things. Both are necessary but as soon as you shift into edit mode you have totally blocked off the flow of creativity and vice versa.

Usually, we need to stay in the creative flow until the great bulk of our song has been written. Then at a later date with an editor's eye we can cut out, add to, or shift around whatever is necessary to make the song truly great. This is most effectively accomplished when we let our songs *rest* until we have forgotten them.

Give it a try. Write your song and then put it away for a couple of weeks or more. Forget about it. After you have let it breathe go back and listen again and quickly make your first impression changes.

You will be pleasantly surprised with the results.

Free Falling - When One Small Thing Can Be BIG!!!

Do you remember a Tom Petty song called "Free Fallin'?"

It was a Top Ten hit back in 1989 (#1 on the US Rock Charts).

If you're not old enough to remember that far back you might recall Tom Cruise singing it in the movie *Jerry Maguire*.

"I'm Freeeeeeeee... free fallin'...."

Still not ringing a bell?

Rolling Stone Magazine listed it as #177 on their list of "The 500 Greatest Songs of All Time."

Even today if I am listening to a classic radio station while driving and that song comes on – oh yeah – I *still* crank it up!

Writing it

I love the story Tom Petty tells about how he and co-writer Jeff Lynne were hanging out on that fateful "Free Fallin'" songwriting day. Tom Petty had started playing a riff on his guitar and humming a tune. Jeff Lynne digs what he is hearing and asks Petty to put some lyrics to it so Mr. Petty starts singing the words from the now famous first verse and basically wrote two verses right then and there.

Jeff Lynne, sensing something cool was beginning to take shape says, "take it up an octave at the chorus."

Petty replies, "What should I say?"

Lynne says, "Say 'I'm free falling'."

So Petty wails out, "I'm freeeeeeeeeeeeeee, free falling....."

Bam! And the rest, as they say, is history.

Octave

Jeff Lynne's contribution of "take it up an octave" is brilliant. Imagine the chorus of that song down an octave in the same place where the verse is being sung. Can you hear it? It just sits there without any *pow*. The verse is still cool and the chorus lyric is still wonderful but the song just sits there. And a song that just sits there, dies.

It's such a small suggestion, "take it up an octave." But it's such a HUGE contribution.

The opening verses of the song move very nicely and paint wonderful pictures without anything added but when the lyric "I'm freeeeee" hits at the chorus up an octave, the song completely *explodes.*

It becomes powerful and irresistible. And has one of the best sing-a-long choruses of its time. *"Take it up an octave."* Brilliant!

Small things

It is amazing how one small thing, one tiny suggestion, like taking the chorus up an octave can be the difference between a song being a classic hit or simply being an obscure musical illustration.

What form of art are you currently working on? Are you writing a song? Are you composing a piece of music or painting a picture? Maybe you are in the studio producing a track.

Whatever you are doing right now, take a step back. Step outside of your feelings of attachment to what you have been working on and try to view it objectively. Is there *one thing* you could change – maybe a small thing – that could be the difference between it being merely a *good* piece of work and becoming a *great* piece of work that reaches out and grabs the masses?

Collaboration

One of the things I think is important for us writers to recognize in the Tom Petty and Jeff Lynne "Free Fallin'" story is that it is a wonderful illustration of *collaboration*.

One of collaboration's great values is that a collaborator will see things you don't see. He or she will look at a work differently than you and will be able to offer a unique perspective. Ideas and suggestions we would never think of like "take it up an octave" will come from a collaborator.

I think I have collaborated with about thirty different writers in the last few years. Are you collaborating with someone right now? If you are not, give it a try. Test the waters and see what can happen. Who knows, you may be just one small octave jump away from writing a #1 hit song.

Maybe the one small thing you need to do is find a collaborator.

Sometimes one small thing makes a big, BIG difference.

Somethin' 'Bout a Truck (Breaking Rules)

There was a song that not too long ago hit #1 on the Country music charts called "Somethin' 'Bout a Truck."

It is performed by a guy named Kip Moore. Take a minute and look it up on the web. Give it a listen. I'll wait.

Cool, huh?

This song amazes me for many reasons.

First of all it makes me nod an approving smile because it's simply a cool song with great vibe and paints a fun picture of life.

Secondly, I am impressed and somewhat baffled by this song because it breaks a few of the fundamental rules of hit songwriting.

Song Form

When I am giving someone advice on how to write a hit song I will *not* tell them to use "Somethin' 'Bout a Truck" as an example of hit songwriting *form*.

Why? Because the largest percentage of hit songs in the last few decades have used some variation of this following song form:

Verse 1
Chorus
Verse 2
Chorus
Bridge
Chorus

In songwriting workshops you will often hear this referred to this as the ABABCB song form or formula. You will also hear that you should never write more than two verses before you get to the first chorus. And writing just one verse before your chorus is even better.

If you analyze the top forty hit songs in any popular genre (Pop, Rock, Country, RnB) you will discover the vast majority of these hits adhere to this songwriting form (give or take an intro, pre-chorus or "turn" section).

The song "Somethin' 'Bout a Truck," however, breaks this songwriting formula *and breaks it big time.*

It has four – FOUR – verses before it ever gets to the chorus. FOUR!!! You simply don't do this in hit songwriting – or do you? This particular song *feels* like it only has three verses before the chorus because the fourth verse is sung up an octave from the previous verses. This higher vocal gives the song a huge *lift* at verse four. (The "lift" is usually saved for the chorus in popular songwriting.)

But writing three verses is *still* too many before some kind of chorus - isn't it?

Captivating

I don't know why this song works so well with *four verses* before the chorus, but it does. Maybe it's because each verse builds and becomes more exciting. Maybe it's because the lyric is captivatingly crafted and draws the listener so deep into the story that you feel as if you are actually sitting right there with the characters.

Maybe the song works because Kip Moore's vocal is perfect for the mood and subject line in this song or maybe it works because the production attitude is flawless.

Most likely it works because all of those above factors are spot on in their delivery as well as in their craft.

Truth be told, I'm not really sure why this song works so wonderfully well when breaking such a huge songwriting rule... but it does.

Rules

I will continue to go on preaching the use of popular song writing form as I have in the past. I will strongly suggest what to use and what not to use. I will go on telling people to never ever put four verses before their first chorus and if they do it will probably kill their chances of getting their song cut.

But I will also need to add an amendment to my lecturing. And that is this: *Sometimes the coolest music of all, the music that really captures our imagination, grabs us by the you-know-what and takes us on a pure pleasure ride is the music that takes all of the rules and shoves 'em!*

So go! Go and write within the parameters of craft developing and fine tuning your skill to communicate your message through an accepted set of metrics. But when inspiration strikes, *chuck 'em all and follow the muse*.

She may lead you some place totally new, unexpected and ultimately cool.

Break the rules.

Meh! I Have Nothing to Say (Songwriting Frustration)

Meh

I tried to start writing a blog post this morning. Everything I wrote sounded like, "Meh." All my words just sat dead on the page. I tried to write a pop song a little later and actually recorded it on my hand-held recorder. But when I listened back, before I even got to the chorus I clicked off the recorder, laid it down on the coffee table and said, "Meh."

Does this ever happen to you?

By then it was about lunch time so I made a sandwich and flipped on CNN. I kid you not, every CNN story was pretty much, "meh."

I decided to bag the songwriting. After finishing my sandwich I went down to my studio to work on some tracks for a TV show.

Slide

The tracks I needed to record for this particular TV show were deep-south swampy-blues tracks. I broke out my guitar and plugged it into an amp. I grabbed a *slide* (I don't actually have a real *slide* for my guitar so I was using an old spark-plug socket).

I began playing a bunch of different slide guitar riffs. I fired up my DAW, opened up a couple of audio tracks and let it rip. I spent the next couple of hours just recording various slide guitar riffs using different guitar sounds.

It was now about 3 o'clock in the afternoon. I pressed play and listened to my last couple hours of slide-guitar riffage.

Meh. Concluding that I suck, I shut down the studio.

Upstairs

I decided, however, I would give songwriting one more shot. From about three-thirty in the afternoon until eight in the evening I wrote two new song "starts." (A song *start* for me is writing at least a verse and chorus with both lyric and music).

I recorded each of them on my hand-held recorder.

I then decided to let the songs simmer while I made myself a dinner salad. After consuming my makeshift salad concoction of romaine, diced apples and tomatoes, peas, blue cheese crumbles and croutons with a bit of virgin olive oil and some fresh ground pepper - anything but meh - I went back into my living room, picked up my recorder and gave both of my new songs a listen.

Meh and meh.

...again I ask, does this ever happen to you?

Pirate Radio

Fairly frustrated with myself but not wanting spiral into any kind of depression about my obvious lack of talent nor stir up any more anxiety about never again being able to make any money from my musical dribble, I poured myself a scotch and put the movie *Pirate Radio* into my DVD player.

After a couple of hours of laughs I fell asleep on the couch.

The next thing I know my wife is waking me up and asking if I'd had a little "accident." Evidently, I had fallen asleep on the couch with my scotch glass in hand and spilled it all over myself.

Half asleep and obviously tired I looked at my "accident," looked at her, and simply said, "Meh!"

Morning

The next morning it was a new day and I had a skip in my step and a song in my heart. At least that's how I felt. I was raring and ready to do some serious damage in the studio as well as with my songwriting.

After my prerequisite bowl of cereal and cup of coffee I headed into the studio.

Before I started any new projects I thought I'd take a moment and flip on my recorders so I could listen to yesterday's "meh" just for laughs.

Surprisingly all three of my songs sounded good. They need tweaking and rewrites but they were darn decent blueprints. I decided to listen to my slide guitar tracks as well. Bingo! I'm a freakin' genius (I like to tell myself that sometimes because no one else ever will.) They sounded *really* cool too! I was pretty sure I got at least two tracks worthy of making into something from yesterday's slide session. Sweet!

Does this ever happen to you?

It happens to me a lot. Too many times to mention.

Why am I telling you this?

So that you don't ever throw anything away.

Your "meh" songs may be much better than you think.

Takeaways (Chapters 26 – 32)

1. Songs in Film and TV foreground music are most often used to support one particular scene or emotion.

2. Film and TV foreground song lyrics should stick to painting one lyrical scene.

3. Background or source music in Film and TV need not adhere to the "paint one scene only" rule as those songs are used for vibe with the lyrics barely heard.

4. When writing and producing in the style of a known artist be careful not to plagiarize.

5. When producing in a particular artist's genre steep yourself in their style. Study and deconstruct the songs to better write and produce in their vibe.

6. Try to find multiple artists within any particular genre to study for a broader scope of style.

7. Practice using the lyric writing technique of visualization. See the scenes and stories in your mind before you write.

8. Write and then rewrite.

9. Practice the technique of writing quickly and letting go. Log your new creations and then put them away for a few weeks before rewriting.

10. Try to identify "one small thing" you can change to make your music better.

11. Take on a collaborator to help you *see* in your music what you cannot. A collaborator brings new perspectives.

12. Follow the rules of songwriting format. And then break them.

13. Don't throw away your bad music. Listen to it again on another day with fresh ears. It may not be as bad as you think.

14. When you are frustrated – work anyway. Even if you don't write or produce a masterpiece you will be sharpening your skills and honing your craft.

The Top 5 Personality Traits Needed to Consider Pursuing a Career in Songwriting

After years of research and tons of personal experience, after many long wine-soaked nights with hundreds of songwriter and composer friends from Nashville to LA and beyond, after contemplating whether or not I should blow smoke up your dress or tell you the cold, hard truth... after the rise and after the fall, after the lovin' and after all the happy-ever-afters have drifted to the rafters... I have reached the conclusion that there are five main personality traits needed if you want to consider pursuing a career in songwriting.

Are you ready?

Here they are.

The Top 5 Personality Traits needed to pursue a career in songwriting:

5. No matter how hard you try, you can't "not write" songs.
4. No matter what you do in an attempt to quit writing, you still can't "not write" songs.
3. You are addicted to songwriting, you can't "not write."
2. Even with no pen, paper, computer or guitar your mind is

making up songs - you can't stop it.
1. You can't "not write!"

Any questions?

Okay, I'm on a roll.

Here are the Top 5 habits of a professional songwriter:

5. You write songs every day.
4. You write songs every week.
3. You write songs when you don't feel like writing songs.
2. You write some very average songs.
1. You re-write your songs.

Happy songwriting!

Disclaimer: Take my Top 5 lists with a grain of salt and maybe a margarita. After all, I am not a psychologist, sociologist, nor am I a rocket scientist. I am just a songwriter and my opinion is highly subjective.

Writer's Roadblock

A short story...

Back in my day I used to walk twenty-five miles to school through three feet of snow in the dark. It was uphill both ways and I loved it! No, I wasn't barefoot. I had cardboard for shoes held onto my shivering feet with mere rubber bands - and I loved it! My skin would crack and peel. Sometimes blood and pus would ooze out my open wounds as I sat through Mrs. McKendrick's penmanship class. It was painful, it hurt, but I loved it!

Yeah, back then – back in the day - you had to be tough as nails, fit as a fiddle and sharp as a tack just to survive. But we loved it. There was no swanky panky Starbucks, no mamby pamby cuppachino, no smart phone or GPS to help us if we got lost.

If we were lost without coffee, we were simply lost without coffee - and we loved it. And this so called reality TV stuff of today? Hell, you don't know what reality is until you've starred down a twelve foot tall mama grizzly, foaming at the teeth, just dying for some morning chew, with nothing but a Boy Scout knife in your pocket to protect yourself. Talk about your virtual video game – yeah, we *lived* those games. And we loved it!

Confession

The above story is not true. As you may have guessed it is an absurd exaggeration, a tall tale. But it can also be helpful.

Sometimes when I sit down to write a song I am absolutely blank. Even after spending twenty or thirty minutes brainstorming every idea I can think of, all I am left with are a few meaningless words and phrases halfheartedly scratched upon a motionless piece of foreboding paper.

It is then that I once again flirt with believing those unwanted guests who live in my mind. Those voices who taunt me every time my muse reaches some roadblock trying to convince me of what, at least in that moment, I already know. That I suck! And that I have no good ideas whatsoever to write about and never will.

It is at this precise moment that I always summon up an old friend (this friend also lives in my mind). Her name is "absurdity." She always waltzes into the room and onto my paper or my laptop with a beautifully boisterous bag of stupid stories, whimsical antidotes, ridiculous rhymes and ludicrous lies.

I began to follow her around as she playfully leads me past her untamed unicorns riding railway rainbows toward three-headed toads hopping down cloud-paved roads high in some sky. She takes me to a place where castles have hands that grip damsels in distress. Or gently ushers me down quiet paths filled with peaceful, still waters and long, lazy days.

Most of where she leads me is utterly useless as far as writing music goes but she always brings a smile to my face and makes me laugh out loud. With her I am always having fun again, feeling the joy of creativity and beginning to imagine all of the adventures and journeys we can take together.

I am loose. I am inspired. I feel good. I am free again and ready to write.

Sometimes making up an exaggerated story about nonsensical stuff or telling a tall tale is a great way to break through creative blockage.

Dropping Needles

I confess. I can't help myself.

I write lyrics, titles and ideas for songs *every day*.

A shrink would probably tell me I am addicted to writing songs.

Or label me a workaholic.

Maybe I am. I don't know.

Most of my song ideas are not "keepers." They are pencil sharpeners so that when a keeper idea comes along I am good and ready to write.

I call my lyric writing time "dropping needles." (No, it is not a drug reference)

Haystack Files

So, what's does the phrase "dropping needles" mean? When I have a project I am writing for I will skim through the hundreds of lyric ideas I have logged over the previous weeks and months searching for that one "needle in the haystack." That diamond in the rough. The true gem or nugget of an idea that could, indeed, be developed and crafted to fit perfectly with the artist or music project I am producing.

My haystack files are also helpful for those times when I have a project that needs to be completed in a timely fashion. If I have to start creating new ideas from scratch sometimes the stress of a fast approaching deadline will cause me to go straight into *edit mode* which all but destroys my creative process.

I've already touched upon the difference between creative thinking and thinking like an editor in previous chapters. Allow me to expound a little more on that difference.

Professional creativity is like taking notes while daydreaming. It is like standing just outside your imagination and reporting on it as you watch each scene unfold. Editing on the other hand is much more like correcting a student's journalism assignment. You put a lot of red pen marks on the paper, scratch a few things out and then give a few suggestions for a rewrite.

While editing you need to be in *detail mode* cognizant of errors and hyper aware of how a particular audience will perceive your vision. While being creative you need to be in *free flow* form. Loose, agile, letting anything and everything in your mind take you wherever it wants to travel. Being creative is like following paths forged by some unseen force outside of your own consciousness.

The anxiety of meeting a deadline or needing to be highly creative very quickly can kill that joyful daydreaming bliss. It can lock tight the doors to your muse in an instant. I do not believe creativity and editing can coexist in the same moment. That is not to say they can't work together in the same room.

Highly skilled people who have mastered their craft can jump back and forth between creativity and editing mode with great success. I, however, am not one of those people. The stress of a mandatory deadline can easily block all pathways to Miss Creative and she will not want to show up on my front porch, asking me to come out and play. She will just ride her tricycle right on by and park her lemonade stand elsewhere.

This is why I spend some time each day "dropping needles."

Right for Co-writes

I have been doing this for years. I keep my lyrics in annual haystack files labeled by year, à la "New Lyric ideas 2014." Inside of each year's folder are documents. One for each month of that folder's particular year.

Every day or evening when I sit down to drop some needles I feel no stress. I am able to quickly brainstorm and log quite a few ideas. In a two hour session I will usually get five lyric ideas each consisting of one verse and one chorus. I don't try to write anymore of the song than that. There is no need to finish anything unless my idea wants me to finish it. Sometimes the song ideas insist on finishing themselves but most are just happy being solid ideas I can refer to when needed.

They are also quite handy to have lying around when I have an unexpected co-write. I can quickly scan through my haystack files and grab five or ten song ideas to present to any co-writer. This can really take the pressure off of a co-writing session which is good because it reduces stress and leads to a more creative environment. You want your co-writer to be as loose and mentally agile as you are.

So there you have it. Dropping needles in my haystack files is part of my process.

I don't know if this is how anyone else writes songs. It's just one of the ways that has been very successful for me.

Time to go drop some needles.

Failing Quickly

Songwriting

Sometimes songwriting baffles me because I can't figure out which songs of mine are good and which ones are not so good. There is great benefit in being able to discern fairly quickly the good ones from the bad. Let me explain.

One of the great challenges I've been plagued with as a songwriter is the unfortunate reality that along with a few good songs I will always write some very *average* songs. Writing an average song in and of itself is not a bad thing. Every songwriter does it. It is part of the process – it is practice.

The problem for me was I had fallen into the habit of spending days, weeks, even months doing numerous rewrites trying to make my mediocre songs sound better. Don't get me wrong, I think that rewriting is a good and necessary thing to do to perfect our craft. It is often how we write great songs. My bugaboo was I could not recognize that these particular songs were *never* going to get much better. They were in the category of what I would refer to as *very average idea* songs.

But I would try. I would try with all of my creative might to coddle and fix these little babies of mine. Hour after hour I would toss and toil, striving with every ounce of skill and craft I could muster to make them acceptable. It never worked. They never became magical.

What's worse is I would do this at the expense of working on some really good songs I had also written. My subconscious thinking was probably something along the lines of "my good songs already sound pretty cool so I can leave them alone. They'll be okay. I'll spend all my time trying to kick my dopey creations up a few notches."

What a colossal waste of time.

It finally dawned on me that I was eating up twenty or more hours each and every week trying to make a bad song sound good. This practice was leaving me with only a couple of hours left to try to make my good songs *great*. I started to ask myself, "What if I simply toss the average songs and spend those twenty extra hours trying to turn my really good songs into *hits*?"

Ah Ha

As soon as I put this new process into practice I began compiling handfuls of songs that were pretty darn good. I was becoming much more efficient. I would still write mediocre songs but now I was developing a brand new skill of recognizing their averageness and letting them go away into the netherworld before they ate up all my time. In other words, I was developing the skill of *failing quickly*.

In Peter Sims brilliant book *Little Bets* he gives numerous examples of people who have had tremendous amounts of success by mastering the art of *failing quickly*. Some of these people are founders of incredibly successful corporations.

What these successful people do is take *little bets* or *little risks* with their business ideas. If their little bets don't work they simply discard them as lessons learned and move quickly on to the next *little bet*. Companies from Hewlett Packard to Google to Pixar to even comedian Chris Rock have perfected this process to great reward.

Thomas Edison, after failing over 1000 times in trying to invent the light bulb said, "I have successfully discovered 1000 ways to *not* make a light bulb." I like that. Thomas Edison took a lot of little bets until one finally paid off.

The trick for me in songwriting is to recognize *quickly* that what I have written might be an okay song but it will probably not be a great song no matter what I do. Then let it go and move on to something new. Some new *little bet*.

Quickly

I like the phrase *failing quickly,* although when we let our ordinary songs go we have not really failed. We have actually spent a few hours practicing, sharpening our skills as writers and grown our craft of recognizing the good from the not so good. It's a win-win-win.

Learning to fail quickly and move onto something potentially better is a valuable skill to develop. Your great songs will thank you and you will increase your odds of discovering something truly magical.

Connecting the Dots

Do you spend your life in a cubicle? Or have you quite possibly parked your mind in a metaphorical cubical? Are you living in a box? Do you ever get outside your four walls and walk down the street eyeing the dancing birds as they improvise their daily songs?

Do you ever take that extra step out of your own world and walk into the world of someone else? Have you ever bought a homeless person a sandwich and then sat and listened to their story?

Songwriting and music production can be isolating. Sitting alone behind a computer or in front of a keyboard while waiting for Lady Muse to make her grand appearance can shrink our world view and deplete our real life resources leaving us dry and uninspired.

If we are isolated too much of the time we will have very little experience with which to feed the muse. We will have trouble *connecting the dots* because we have very few dots to connect.

Blues

Have you ever heard the saying *"you can't sing the blues unless you've lived the blues?"* I'm not sure I believe the literal translation of this particular phrase but I will concede it is quite difficult to sing the blues (or write, or play authentic blues) unless you have allowed yourself to at least be a witness to some real life blues.

How can we expect to write about someone's utter agony unless we bear witness to another human crying out in desperation from a broken heart, a broken life or a broken body?

If we have not experienced this kind of pain will most likely only write what we *think* that kind of desperation encompasses. We need to *feel* their pain to even begin to understand that kind of hurt. We need to cradle the aching person in our arms, rocking them gently as we search and scour our souls for comforting words to say. Sometimes discovering there are no words of comfort or healing, no wisdom that can mend.

Then, and only then, will we have a shot at accurately conveying their tragedy to others.
None of us can expect to write truly authentic blues until we have experienced these emotions deep down in those recesses of our souls. Until we ache and moan for another's travesty our music won't truly ache and moan.

Until we have been a witness we will not be able to "connect the dots" because we will not yet have acquired all of the emotional "dots" needed for full and complete expression.

And it's not just the blues. The same experience or witnessing is needed to authentically express any musical genre's emotion. Can someone truly produce great dance music if they have never been inside of a club and felt the pulse of the drums, the weight of the bass in their chest and the flow of the crowd? Maybe one in a million.

Experience life

My advice to you (and to me) is to go *live life*.

Go to a coffee shop and watch two little kids in their pink and purple raincoats. Yeah, those two precocious kids whose mother is not watching because she is busy telling the cashier she was positive there were still eight dollars left in her wallet.

Watch those little cuties as they walk over to the coffee kiosk filled with bags of Pike Place Roast. See them twirl around in a child's uninhibited dance of pure joy and utter freedom. Feel their mom's frantic panic as she turns from the counter just in time to see their errant arms flailing into the kiosk causing a cascade of bagged coffee to tumble and scatter on the cafe floor.

Then, if you are not helping the mother pick up the spilled coffee bags, scan the faces of the other customers. See some of them giggle "oh, such adorable children," and watch others shake their heads in disgust muttering, "what a horrible mother."

Once you have done this - write about it. Put it in a song. Give it a tune.

Or go down to the local park. Smell the flowers, the dogwood trees, the freshly cut grass. Bend over and run your fingers through the grass. Notice the blue sky above and the heat of the sun as it blankets the top of your head. Put your hand in your hair and feel the sun's warmth.

Take a look at the people there. Watch the kids running free and chanting their sing-a-long songs. Look at their little neon green tennis shoes with the Velcro strips. Observe their parents as they chat. What are they talking about?

See the college kids playing with their Budweiser Frisbee. Listen to the Frisbee as it whizzes by through the air. Look at the creepy old man sitting on the bench near the swings. Why is he wearing an overcoat on a hot, sunny afternoon? Ask yourself, "should I call the cops?"

Now go home and write about it. Describe what your senses are experiencing. Give this local park scene a melody and a title. Paint this park's *furniture* in your lyrical phrases.

Connect the dots

Real life experiences are the dots we will take back to our writing rooms and figure out how to connect.

You've got a lot to write about even with only those few everyday-type experiences. Maybe you will write a song about the pain of divorce. Maybe you write a song about the neighborhood gossips. About how what goes around, comes around. Maybe it's a children's song that you write. About dancing and singing with that wonderful carefree joy only a child knows.

The point is that we need to smell a lot of roses, and dandelions, and chickweed and baby diapers if we want to be creative. If we want have dots to connect and if we desire to paint beautiful new works of art, we need to go dot shopping.

Don't get me wrong. There is no substitute for sitting in your studio and doing the work.
But there is also no substitute for getting out of your studio and living life.

12 Notes

There are only twelve notes in modern music.

Look it up.

Whether it is Rock, Jazz, Rap, Country or Opera - there's just twelve.

Yup,12.

Twelve of them funny little circles with lines and flags all dancing together on a fence.

Here's some advice... Don't be a music snob.

If music makes someone feel something then it is fine. It may not be your particular cup of tea but it is just fine. We all need to get over ourselves, our puffed up opinions and our "this is better than that" spouting off.

It's time to take a deep breath.

Segregation Rant

It has been my observation that musicians can be some of the most snobbish and non-inclusive people in the world when it comes to their love/hate relationship with various styles and genres of music.

Stop it!

If this describes you (or me) then we are doing ourselves a great disservice as artists by building walls and ruling out certain types of music we consider somehow beneath us. We are also disabling those whom we are mentoring.

There are only twelve notes. Seriously, how different can the various genres of music really be?

Every style of popular modern music uses those same notes (except quarter-tone music which I'll bet you don't listen to anyway).

Maybe even more importantly, listen to or read the interviews of successful musicians and artists. They are rarely music snobs. Most have a great appreciation for a wide variety of styles. Could this be key to their great success?

Steep

If you are a metal guy or girl one of the best things you can do for yourself is to find a music style that you detest - maybe some old Pat Boone stuff - and listen to it.

Steep yourself in it. Ask yourself why so many millions of people love this type of music and don't stop your study of it until you find the answers.

If you are solely a Hip-hop Rap Dude (or Dudette) or a Bebop Jazzer who hates most everything else, go and grab every Waylon Jennings record you can get your hands on and dig deep into it. And then go and download fifteen Sarah McLachlan songs and live with them until you completely understand why she has millions of fans.

Do not stop your daily listening to Waylon and Sarah until you can truly *feel* why so many love those particular artists.

You think I'm exaggerating, don't you? I'm not.

You will probably resist doing this. You don't want to listen to stuff you don't like. You think this is an exercise for someone else - not you.

Do it anyway.

Public Enemy

I've told this story before, so if you've already heard it please bear with me.

When Rap music was starting to gain mainstream traction back in the late 80s I wasn't hip to it. I didn't get it. But then again I had never really listened to it. I decided I needed to educate myself so I went down to my local record store (remember those?) and bought a Public Enemy cassette. I know, right? It was baptism by Chuck D and Flavor Flav.

I listened to the cassette *Fear of a Black Planet* over and over again. I dug deep into the rhythms, the lyrics and into the melodies. I opened myself up as wide as I could to the experience because I somehow knew that I needed to stretch, to learn, to understand, to *feel* what this Rap thing was.

Hip Hop and Rap will most likely never be my forte in writing and producing but steeping myself in Public Enemy way back in the day was the beginning of a deep appreciation for both the musicality of Rap and a social awareness of a culture and lifestyle I was not privy to nor a part of. I grew tremendously.

I have repeated this process with many artists and styles of music. To this day I continue to use this discipline I stumbled upon those many years ago to grow and stretch myself.

Do you get it? Do you understand?

Why?

It does not matter if you or I like a particular artist or genre of music. In fact, the more we dislike something the more beneficial it is to go and learn from it.

Although we may never fall in love with a particular kind of music we will begin to understand why other people like it. And those insights will benefit us in all aspects of our career. Those answers will have a profound effect on growing our music, our business sense and our marketing skills.

Now do it. Go and grow.

And so will I.

Amen

Takeaways (Chapters 33 – 38)

1. Break through writer's block by inviting the silly and absurd into your imagination.

2. Taking things too seriously can sometimes hinder our creativity. Humor can make us loose again unlocking the creative muse.

3. Write every day. Even if it is just a verse and a chorus. In fifty days you will have fifty ideas to sort through. A few of them might be great.

4. Collecting and documenting your ideas will give you a great resource to draw upon and bring to the table in any collaborative effort.

5. Don't dwell too long on an average idea. Let it go and create something new.

6. Spend the majority of your time turning your great ideas into magic.

7. Experience life. Observe life. A great way to collect song ideas is to get out and observe the world you live in and the people who inhabit it.

8. Interact with people. If you can compassionately empathize with people you will be able to write about situations you yourself may never experience.

9. Find a type of music you do not like and then steep yourself in it. You will grow musically and better understand what people connect with.

10. Uncover the main reasons why so many people enjoy a genre you don't care for. This practice will grow your marketing sensibilities.

Stuff Changes

Stuff changes. Whether we like it or not.

It's hard to keep up. But those of us who are trying to make our living in the music business must. We must keep up with the new ways our music is being marketed and delivered. We must educate ourselves on the present and future media communication formats so we can better see how to position ourselves to make a buck.

We may not want to but we *must*. Things are changing with us or without us.

I know many of you don't like change. I am still going through withdrawals because I am one of those people who deeply enjoyed holding a newspaper in my hands while sipping my morning java. And I, too, am one of those nerds who loves the smell of the pages in a new book. I like the way I can write on and underline things within those magical ink filled pages. But alas, soon most books as I know and love them will be gone, giving way to some cold, lighted, sterile pad or tablet I will clutch in my darkened bedroom late at night.

Spotify and other Cloudy things

We musicians need to know about such things as the possibility of iTunes fading into oblivion and newcomers like Spotify, Amazon, Pandora or whatever is next taking its place. Why? One reason is money. Price structures (how we are paid) are changing as fast as new technologies are being developed. And you can bet there are many fingers already trying to grab their piece of the emerging

Cloud pie. Laws are being rewritten. Corporate deals are being made. We need to educate ourselves on the evolving entertainment environments if we want to be equipped to fight for our right to get more than a few crumbs from underneath the tycoon's table.

Blockbuster and Vinyl

My Blockbuster Video store is gone. There used to be one about a mile from my house. A bunch of people were employed there not too long ago. But now they are all gone. Their jobs have vanished. DVDs are all but gone. Netflix, Amazon Prime, DVRs and watching TV online or on our smart phones are all grappling for our viewing dollars. I'll bet Blockbuster Video didn't want Netflix and Red Box to happen. But they did. Stuff changes.

I still have over four thousand vinyl albums. Yup, vinyl records. Remember - those Frisbee-like things. I love my vinyl. Back in the day, in the 70s, we used to take all of our money and buy the best speakers we could afford along with the best stereo system we could find. We would then put our new purchases in the main living space in our house or apartment.

When our favorite artist would put out a new record we would go down to Tower Records, pay the man, bring home our new record, put it on the stereo and listen to it all the way through. We would pour over the liner notes and memorize not only the lyrics but the writers and producers and engineers and musicians' names. It was pure bliss. It was an event.

LPs were front and center stage in our lives. We bought them. We owned the music. We invited our friends to come over and listen. We had parties. It was one of our three or four main sources of entertainment. How many entertainment options are there these days? Hundreds? Thousands?

Today you might own some iTunes files but tomorrow you won't. You probably won't actually *own* any new music. It will be in the cloud. You will pay a monthly fee for access to the greatest music catalogs ever assembled and you will probably do your primary listening on an iPhone or through cheap computer speakers.

Music will no longer be front and center stage in your life. It probably already isn't. You will listen to it while you are doing something else. It will serve mostly as a *background track* to the rest of your life.

And because music in the new world is much more of a backdrop than it used to be, artists, producers and songwriters will probably be paid less for it than they were just a few short years ago. The good news for us music creators is that our music will be used in hundreds of additional places and in ways we never dreamed of in the years to come. What that means is that for those who successfully navigate the many sources of new revenue streams, there will indeed be plenty of money to be made.

Stuff is changing. Whether you and I like it or not.

Horses

Imagine living 120 years ago. Back when your main means of travel was riding a horse, or a horse and buggy, or a covered wagon. Back then your horse was everything to you. Sometimes your very life depended upon your horse. You loved that horse. You took great care of it. You fed it well and made sure it was always safe and secure. Then one day someone invented – gasp – a car.

All of a sudden this noisy, smelly, smoky car was driving down your horse-traveled dusty road. You probably didn't like the car because it terrified your horse. It agitated him and he couldn't eat or sleep.

Then more cars came and suddenly someone wanted to put paved roads through your town. Soon they built more paved roads and then freeways. The concrete hurt your horse's feet. You didn't like the way things were changing but you couldn't stop it.

I'm here to tell you today your horse is going away. The new "cars" have arrived, the Internet roads have been paved and your music is now traveling to its destination in a different way. You may not like it but you need to educate yourself to it, especially if you want to capitalize on the possible new revenue streams.

We can hide our heads in the sand if we want to.

But there is a new wave crashing upon our musical shores…

Stuff changes.

Digital Fingerprinting

Up until just recently the songs you may have written and placed in a TV show or a film have been identified for royalty purposes by their title. You may get paid on a licensing fee for the use of your Master Recording but traditionally the other way you get paid is from monies your performing rights organization collects for you from per-negotiated performance royalty rates.

You get credit for your song being used on a TV show because someone in that particular TV show's production company filled out what is called a *cue sheet*. This cue sheet is then filed with your PRO (ASCAP, BMI, SESAC, SOCAN, etc...). Your PRO then sends you a check for the royalty amount owed to you after they have collected it.

A cue sheet lists the title of every piece of music that was played in a particular TV show. It also lists the amount of time each piece of music was played. In addition, for each piece of music on a cue sheet the writers and publishers' information will be listed, along with the performing rights organization affiliation and whether it was used as foreground or background music, as well as any other pertinent information.

A typical song of mine on a cue sheet might read something like this:

SWANKY NETWORK TV SHOW
Title: My Beautiful Song
:53 sec.
Writer: Dean Krippaehne
Publisher: Dean's Big Time Publishing Company
PRO: ASCAP

One of the things many songwriters and producers have done in the past in hopes of increasing their opportunities for song placements is to sign their songs to multiple "non-exclusive" music libraries under different song titles. This is a practice called *re-titling*.

The non-exclusive agreement gives the signing library (Dean's Big Time Publishing Company) the right to pitch a song (My Beautiful Song) and collect the publishing royalties and licensing fees for placements on that song *title*. They do not collect royalties and fees on this song if it has been placed elsewhere by another company under a *different title*.

Because they (Dean's Big Time Publishing Company) do not own the *exclusive* publishing rights to the song with a *non-exclusive* contract, the writer is free to sign that same song elsewhere.

If the writer signs this same song with a second music library (we'll call this library Publisher #2), Publisher #2 needs be a non-exclusive publisher as well. When Publisher #2 signs the song and starts pitching it to TV shows they must give the song a *different title* so that when it gets placed on a TV show and logged in a cue sheet the PRO will know that any monies collected must go to Publisher #2 and not Dean's Big Time Publishing Company.

Are you with me?

While Dean's BTPC would have titled the song "My Beautiful Song," Publisher #2 might title that same song "My Very Pretty Song." Same song, different title. That way when "My Beautiful Song" shows up on a cue sheet the PRO will know to send the royalties to Dean's BTPC and if "My Very Pretty Song" shows up on a cue sheet the PRO will know to send the royalties to Publisher #2.

This practice of re-titling and signing the same song with multiple non-exclusive publishers has been quite common over the last many years. Again, the idea from the writer's perspective is the more companies pitching his or her song (with different titles), the better the writer's odds of securing TV show placements and making big royalty bucks will be.

Those days may be ending.

There is a new practice of tracking songs called "digital fingerprinting." Digital fingerprinting has been tested, tried and is now truly seeping into every aspect of music "performance" reporting. What digital fingerprinting does in essence is take a picture of the audio of your song and store it in some gigantic server database-thingy on the planet Mars - or some place like that.

When your song is played on a TV show (or anywhere - including the planet Mars) its digital fingerprint pops up. It is then logged into a cue sheet and you are paid accordingly.

The sticky part for anyone who has their song re-titled and in multiple music libraries is when the fingerprint of their song comes up and is logged in the database, it will show multiple titles and multiple music publishers as owners. That is a problem.

In other words when "My Beautiful Song" shows up as a digital fingerprint it will be displayed as having both titles "My Beautiful Song" (Dean's Big Time Publishing) and "My Very Pretty Song" (Publisher #2). The question then of course is: *who does the royalty check go to?* Does it go to Dean's Big Time Publishing or Publisher #2?

At first glance it seems like the most obvious solution is to simply ask the TV show's production company or the PRO to call up both music libraries find out which publisher pitched the song. But not so fast.

With millions of songs to track each and every month there will be no phone calling by the PROs or the production company personnel. They simply won't have the time or the inclination to track down all of those titles' rightful owners just so you can get you money. The song will just go on hold (maybe somewhere on Planet Mars) and no one will ever get paid. At least no one will get paid unless they do A LOT of digging and phone calling and tracking on their own. And even then it may take months if not years to get your ten bucks.

And what happens when both of the song's publishers have pitched that very same song to the same show? And they both claim ownership? And what happens when both publishers get angry and decide to sue the Production Company, TV Show and Network?

Enter the Lawyers

When this happens – and it already has – the proverbial "you know what" can hit the fan. Production companies and TV shows in an effort to avoid lawsuits quite probably will no longer accept music from either of the publishing libraries involved. There is also a good chance they will no longer accept songs from the writer of any song named in the lawsuit.

Believe me, these guys do not want litigation of any kind at their doorstep so you don't want to be "that person" who has your song with multiple titles in numerous music libraries.

Does this mean you or I shouldn't sign any of our songs with a non-exclusive library?

Not necessarily.

But if a particular library has too many digital fingerprinting infractions it is possible they could become blacklisted by certain Production Companies, Music Supervisors, TV shows and even Networks. So you want to be aware of who you are signing your songs with and what their reputation is.

(Please note that there are arguments both pro and con in this fingerprinting/re-titling issue. I am only presenting one opinion based on my own personal research, experience and gut feeling.)

Exception

There will, however, continue to be a different kind of non-exclusive contract that is safe in this new digital fingerprinting environment. This particular type of non-exclusive contract is primarily for an artist who signs his or her CD's songs to a music library for the purpose of placing those songs in Film, TV, Video Games and Advertisement Campaigns. The music library has the exclusive right to pitch this music for these purposes and these purposes only.

The artist, however, retains full ownership of his or her music and the rights to sell and collect all of the monies from CD sales, digital downloads and radio airplay.

This type of agreement should be safe. (Disclaimer: I am not a lawyer and this is only my opinion.)

So What Do I Do?

Everyone has to search their own hearts and minds when it comes to signing the same song to multiple music libraries under different titles. I can't make the decision for you. I am only giving you a "heads up" and from where I am observing it looks as if the digital fingerprinting of music is fast upon us and here to stay.

Then again, my whole point may be moot if someone figures out how to put multiple fingerprints on the same song.

Risky Business

Recently I went to the NAB convention in Las Vegas.

The NAB convention is a digital media, broadcasting type thing. It is also definitely related to the Film and TV music production business.

Did I need to go to this conference? Probably not.

Was it a good idea for me to go? Absolutely!

My few days in the desert cost me well over a thousand bucks with the flight from Seattle, hotel room and conference expense.

It was money out of my pocket indeed - money gone. Poof!

But... *sometimes we need to spend a little to make a little.* I wish this wasn't true. I've been searching for a magical money tree for years but have yet to discover it.

Most musicians I know are quite familiar with the money out, more money out, going, going, gone thing. In fact most people I know who have started their own business know the unforgiving truth that you need to spend money to make money.

Pandora

Not too long ago I read that Pandora (Internet Radio) has been losing money every year since they were founded. I don't think it would be much of a stretch to say that after over a decade of losing money Pandora's philosophy is they need to spend money to make money. (In 2011 they had revenues of $130,000,000 and still lost money.)

Who knows whether Pandora's business model will be successful in the long run? Pandora is indeed spending a lot of money in the hopes of making even more. My guess is they are not just foolishly frittering away their dollars. Pandora's spending and risks are most likely well calculated with their options thoroughly weighed so they can make the best decisions possible and position themselves for success.

So, why was it a good idea for me to spend my hard earned money on attending the NAB show in Las Vegas?

It was, in fact, a well calculated risk.

Risk Calculation

The reality is this particular conference was where the heartbeat of my industry was hanging out during its run. I needed to go and learn, get new ideas, discover what everyone else in the digital music business is doing and soak it all in. I needed to network and build relationships with the people who work in and run the companies I am (or hope to be) doing business with.

I had about twenty meetings set up with various people during my week at the conference. I felt that if I connected in a positive way with *five* of those people and their companies the *near term return* on my investment could be at least twenty times greater than the thousand dollars I was forking out. And who knows what the long term return on this investment could be. It quite possibly could be a much greater number.

Could it all flop? Could I gain absolutely nothing from my time at the NAB convention?
In strictly monetary terms the answer is yes. It could flop and I could gain *zippo*. But from a relationship building standpoint and

a knowledge gaining aspect there could be no such thing as a flopped trip.

The *brain* goods I acquired in those few short days are probably equivalent to the education one would get in a PhD program at a major university which would cost substantially more.

So there is no real downside to this expenditure. No real risk. It does have value.

Smackers, Greenbacks and Clams

Those of us who are pursuing music careers, even if we are just a one person business, will all need to dole out some investment bucks from time to time. We will be forced to turn over a few greenbacks and shuck a few clams as they say. Whether it is fifteen dollars on replacing guitar strings or a couple G's on a new orchestra sample library we will need to spend some moolah from time to time.

It's tough. It can hurt. To minimize your risk you will want to do your best, most diligent research and some cautious calculation so you can invest wisely and get the most bang for your buck. If you are smart with your decisions good things will happen.

In the end, investing in any business (and you are a business) is somewhat of a gamble. But if you are talented, work hard at your craft, investigate and learn from others who are farther along the path than you, it can be well worth it.

It takes guts, grit, grime and gumption to get up and go but why not take the risk? This boat we are all sailing on will only float for so long. We might as well stop off at some exotic shores and enjoy a few exciting adventures along the way.

The Ten Commandments and the Music Biz

**Note: Don't let the above title scare you away. For this chapter it doesn't matter what religion you subscribe to or even if you have no religion. You will gain some valuable info and insight into the business of doing music by walking with me through this examination of the historical Ten Commandments.

Let me start by giving a brief one or two sentence summary of each of the Biblical Ten Commandments just to see if anything jumps out at us as a common thread through them all. Then we will look to see if there is something we may be able to learn from these Stone Tablet Etchings that could be applicable to the music biz. Stay with me. Here we go.

1. *I am the Lord thy God. You shall have no other Gods before me.*
This is pretty clear. God is proclaiming to be THEE Big Kahuna. I think it also means we should put God first and foremost in our lives spending time with Him/Her in an ongoing *relationship*.

2. *Don't make up your own "gods."*
Stop worshiping money and success the way Dean Krippaehne sometimes does. Also, this commandment directs us again to value our *relationship* with God.

3. *Don't take the name of God in vain.*
Bam! Value and respect the *relationship* you have with God – don't crap on it. A lot of people think this commandment means "don't swear." It probably does to some degree but I tend to think

it means something far greater. We can dump on God's name just by refusing to love and care for those around us.

This is certainly much more destructive than simply blurting out "goddammit" when the hammer head hits our thumb. In addition, I would submit that there are hundreds of priests and preachers pontificating their own ideas about God every week who are really bashing God's name and distorting God's Truth. (I also happen to think there are thousands who are *not* bashing God's name and are indeed, leading people in Truth.)

Whatever the intended meaning behind this commandment *relationship* is at its core.

4. Keep Holy the Sabbath.
This commandment may be pointing to a particular day or an amount of time each week to keep "holy." Whatever it is referring to the main point is to again, spend your "Sabbath" time in *relationship* with God.

5. Honor your father and mother.
This *doesn't* mean our parents are or were always right. It means we should strive as best we can to have a respectful, caring *relationship* with our parents.

6. Thou shalt not murder.
Don't murder anyone. Human life is valuable. Always be healthy enough in your *relationships* so you don't become so hateful or fearful that you began to consider murder as an option.

7. Do not commit adultery.
Don't screw someone who is married or you will screw up your *relationships*.

8. Thou shalt not steal.
Other peoples stuff is other peoples stuff, not yours. Keep your *relationships* with everyone respectful.

9. Thou shalt not bare false witness.
Don't be a freaking liar! You want to keep honesty central in all your *relationships*.

10. Don't covet thy neighbor's wife or goods, or anything else.

She (or he) may be hot but you need to respect and honor them and their spouse enough to keep your *relationships* pure.

What is the Point?

Do you see it - the word *relationship*? Amazing isn't it? Each one of the Ten Commandments is about *relationships* with others and with God. God really has a theme going on here. Without ever even reading the rest of the Bible I think we can ascertain from all of this that *relationships* were of the utmost importance to God.

Now let's move on and try to relate this to the music biz. If you look closely you will discover that relationships may play a key role in achieving a successful career in music.

The Ten Music Biz Commandments According to Dean

It is in the spirit of the Judeo-Christian Commandments that I now give you the Dean's list. His Top Ten Commandments for the music biz.

1. *Have a good relationship with yourself.*
Take care of yourself. Exercise and eat right. Take care of your psychological and emotional well-being. Don't over indulge in stuff. Get help for your addictions and surround yourself with positive people who can help you grow. Energy comes from a healthy lifestyle. You will need energy to run in this marathon business and you will also be with *yourself* more than any other being on this planet. Take good care of YOU.

2. *Be professional, positive and polite.*
First of all, just be professional in all of your dealings with others. Cross you T's and dot your I's. Do what you say you are going to do and show up on time. Also, be positive and smile. People are

attracted to positive people and repelled by negativity. You can't build a good relationship if you repel people. Lastly, be polite. Two of the most useful and powerful words in the music biz and in life are the words "thank you." If you don't have any manners, grow some.

3. *Ask the Universe for help.*
I don't want to get all hocus-pocus on you but it will behoove you (and me) to engage in a relationship with *all that is.* Whatever you want call it: God, Abba, The Creator, The Universe, The Force...

Think about it. If you have ever looked at any of NASA's space pictures, if you have ever listened to an astrophysicist speak, you are well aware that this universe is massive and that over 99.99% of it remains a complete and utter mystery to all of us. Embrace the mystery and the possibility that there is something out there that can help us down here. Why not - it can't hurt.

4. *Ask other people for help.*
Whether it is songwriting, producing, learning new software, finding a publisher or if it is totally unrelated to the music business, ask other people for help. Most of the time they will want to share what they know with you. Your *relationships* will grow.

5. *Be nice to those people who help you (and also to those who do not help you).*
Thank those who help and offer your help in return... And even those who don't help you - offer your help to them. Build respectful *relationships.*

6. *Get to know your audience.*
Hang out with the people whom you want to reach with your art. Learn what they like, how they talk, what makes them laugh and what makes them cry. Spend time with them in *relationship* and you will learn how to better communicate your music to them. You might even make a new friend or two.

7. *Hang out with the biz folks - buy them a drink (sheesh, buy me a drink).*
It's called networking. Get yourself to the conferences, seminars, workshops or clubs where the people in your business hang out. Strike up a conversation. Buy them a drink, or coffee, or dinner. A lot of people will accept. Trust me. I've done this a lot. Hang with

them and listen to them. People like to be listened to. And if they like the "hang" they will like you. Again, it's called *relationship building*.

8. Be kind to those who are not as far along on the path as you are.
A friend of mine tells a wonderful story about a time back in the 90s when he had a couple hit songs and was sitting on a song-screening panel at a music conference. After his panel was done one of the conference attendees walked up to him, shook his hand, and thanked him for giving a fair and respectful critique of his song.

They struck up a friendly conversation, hung out for awhile and then said their goodbyes. By the mid 2000s this conference attendee had become one of the biggest producers on the planet.

My friend called him up one day to say hello not knowing if the producer would even remember him. Not only did the producer remember my friend, he invited him over to his mansion to hang out and a new business relationship was formed.

Do you think it was a good thing my friend treated this big-time producer with respect and kindness back in the day? You bet! Be kind to everyone. *Relationships.*

9. Get a dog or a cat or a squirrel and take care of them.
Pets are cool. Having to feed, clean up and care for any living thing will help build your *relationship* muscle. The main growth opportunity here is when it is our responsibility to take care of some living, breathing thing we must often meet their needs *first* before we our own needs are met. This strengthens our ability to be more "others-centered" and less self-centered.

10. Share your expertise with others.
You have something to offer other people. Maybe your expertise is not yet in music production or songwriting. It doesn't matter. You have something, probably many things to offer. Maybe you have a lot of experience at being married, or raising kids, or taking care of kittens, or unicorns, or in becoming a better skier or skydiver.

I don't know what it is but you have a lot to offer. Maybe Mr. Big Shot Record A&R Executive does not know how to teach his dog how to sit and roll over but you are an expert in dog training. You can give him your knowledge and start a new *relationship*. Always remember *you* have a lot to offer.

11. Yes, number ELEVEN. This is the hidden commandment. Part of the Music Biz's Dead Sea Scrolls. Are you ready? Here goes…

"Give back to the world."

Wherever you are in your life and whatever level of success you have or have not achieved you can always give back to the world. There will always be someone less fortunate than you. If you are reading this right now you know it is true because there are still millions in the world who cannot even *read*.

Give to them. Feed them, clothe them, shelter them or bring medicine to them. Have a *relationship* with the world. Give to the world and it will give back to you in ways you can't even imagine.

Final Thoughts

In the music biz and in the business of life it is all about *relationships*.

Embrace it.

Lost in Translation

Have you ever written something in an email or made a post on Facebook or Twitter that was taken entirely the wrong way?

I sure have.

Communication is a funny thing. Good communication is a necessary thing. One of the great laments of my life has been watching good people let their relationships unravel because of bad communication.

Recently

Recently I received an email from a long time client whose company is producing a one minute video ad for an international corporation. They asked me if I would write and produce the music for this video.

There was already some "temporary" music in the video. It was a light acoustic piano and pizzicato string piece with a carefree attitude to it. They liked this piece of music but didn't think it had quite the right feel. Here is what they said to me in their email request:

"Attached is a link to the video. The client has reviewed it and it looks good so the video team is going to continue editing. However, they want to replace the existing music with something with a more exciting feel to it."

When I inquired about possibly getting a bit more information or direction per the style of music they were looking for their email reply was:

"We would like the background music to be something more exciting and powerful."

So there you have it. Those were my instructions. I am not kidding. Let us review their description of the kind of music they wanted me to write and produce:

1. Something exciting
2. Something powerful
3. Something that is not carefree piano with pizzicato strings

Question

Given those instructions what kind of music would *you* produce and send to them? What do you think is powerful and exciting? Is it an ESPN type Heavy Metal cue with crunching guitars? Or maybe a tense, action movie trailer type piece? How about a four-on-the-floor fashion, runway-model dance track? Maybe exciting and powerful means something similar to "The Flight of the Bumblebee" or the "Theme from Rocky." Either of those would be exciting and powerful.

Have you decided yet? Me neither.

The obvious answer to this dilemma was I needed more information. I needed to contact the client and try to get a more defined description of what exactly they were looking for.

I always find it tremendously helpful if I can get a client to name two or three songs they think might fit the mood. Then I can use those songs as a style template and try to write and produce something smack dab in middle of their ballpark.

But what if the client gives you no more descriptive clues than, "I want it to be exciting, powerful and have no carefree piano or pizzicato strings?"

I should tell you that I did have one additional clue. I was able to view part of the video and I can tell you that the video was set in a cheery business office and had a slightly whimsical feel to it. I would guess the demographic they were trying to reach was the 25 to 50 year old casual-professional.

Given this additional information I didn't think I should go too far out on the edge genre-wise. No extreme metal, heavy hip-hop or rambunctious hillbilly-country and probably no high-fashion-runway-model-slamming-disco music. My guess is it would be best to stay somewhere in the *middle* of all that.

This above scenario of having very little musical style direction from a client is not at all uncommon in the music business. I am often left trying to *guess* what might work well for a client with little to no specifics to guide me. I think this may happen because the client really doesn't know how to *communicate* what they want in *musical* terms and are asking me (or you) to help *translate* their vision for them.

The Production

So what did I do as I sat down to write and produce something for them?

I punted.

What I mean is I decided to produce a generic peppy pop style piece of music. Something that the artist Pink might do. I would then send it off to the client as a "starting point" knowing they might not like it much but we would at least have a point of reference.

I reasoned that if they didn't like it we would at least have discovered one more thing they *didn't* want and maybe this musical starting point would give them some new language tools to better communicate their vision. (I.e. I was hoping they might respond with something like, "We hated the drums pounding like that, loved the guitars" and/or "We think that the tempo is about right.")

I asked them to give it a listen and then get back to me with further direction.

About an hour later the production company sent me an email saying they liked it and that this piece of music might work but could I "pull out the edgy synthesizer part?" I pulled out the synths, sent them a new version and waited for a response.

To make a long story short, all they wanted after that was a couple more little tweaks and we were done. They were happy. I got lucky.

Translation

Communication is a weird thing. Sometimes you may think it has occurred when nothing has really been communicated at all. It behooves us as creators of music to become students of communication, students of social language and cultivators of relationships. We need to have our sensors up always learning how to decipher any new and unique language our fellow humans may throw our way. We need to be flexible and willing to become familiar in foreign land so that we don't get lost – in translation.

Or... we just need to get lucky.

Diversify

Did your mother ever say to you when you were a kid, "Don't put all your eggs in one basket?"

What did she mean anyway?

I didn't carry a basket back then nor did I have any eggs to put in it.

Hatching a plan

We've all heard the same advice from financial planner types on TV. *Diversify* your portfolio. (I.e. don't put all your eggs in one basket.)

They want us to spread out our investment money between real estate, stocks and bonds and the money market. And if our employer has a matching funds retirement plan the financial planning gurus want us to add to it. Start a self-employment plan or a 401k and always keep some cash on hand they say.

And even *within* the stock or real estate markets most financial advisers will encourage us to diversify by buying into different types of companies or properties. Some advisers will also suggest buying gold, art, antiques and other things that can retain or increase in value.

But why do they want us to diversify?

Why not just dump all of our money into one stock in the stock market and be done with it? That would be easiest thing to do and we wouldn't have to try to figure out all of the other stuff.

The answer in the financial would is that at any given point of time we can see the value of our investment money *rise or fall*. And the objective in diversification is to cover our bases and butts. Usually, when one investment falls in value, another investment type will rise. If we are diversified (or so the theory goes) we will be much more apt to remain financially secure through good times and bad and much less apt to lose all of our assets on one unlucky or ill-advised bet.

So the answer to the "why diversify" question is: *reduction of risk.*

History

Even if you didn't have any money in the stock market, unless you've been living underneath a rock for the last few years you are aware of the stock market crash in 2007-2008. If all of your money was in the market, especially if it was all invested in the companies that took the biggest hits you would have lost a tremendous percentage of the value of your narrowly invested portfolio.

The same is true in real estate. If real estate was the only place you had your money invested during that time you probably took quite a hit, especially if your holdings were only in a places like Las Vegas or Miami.

However, if you had part of you money invested in gold you may have remained fairly stable through these turbulent times because the value of gold soared, nearly tripling during the same time frame of the housing and stock market collapses.

So, financially speaking, diversification can be a pretty good thing.

What about music?

You have probably heard at one time or another from music business folks that you should concentrate on one thing, one talent or skill, and become the very best at it.

Whether it is being a songwriter, a singer, an engineer, a bass player or whatever, the idea is that the road to success is paved with being the very best at whatever it is you do. And the reason for concentrating on just one thing is that it will take most all of your time and most all of your effort to become the very best at it.

I can't argue with that principle. To become the very best at anything you need to give it *all you've got*.

However, many jobs that were once stable and a staple in many industries are now scarce or non-existent. I think there is another side to the "do only one thing" equation, especially in this new day and age where the rapid change in technology is turning not only the music business but most every business upside down.

Back in the Day

Back in the 70's it was pretty easy to make an okay living as a club musician in my city - Seattle. But two things happened that changed all of that. The first big hit to live musicians came with the advent of disco. Almost overnight the disco scene became huge and club owners realized they could pack out a club and only have to pay one person, a DJ, instead of an entire band. This was an easy savings (or profit) of $100,000 or more per year for a small club owner. So it was natural that this new economic reality would drive club owners toward DJs.

The second big hit to the live musician in my corner of the world came with the rise in popularity of karaoke. Again, instead of paying for an entire band to perform the club owners could simply pay one karaoke host to run the show, generating tens of thousands in additional savings (or bottom line revenues) each year.

If you were a gigging musician in the 1980s you took a huge hit in both the availability of gigs and the amount of money you were being paid. Even in my little town of Seattle I saw hundreds of musicians forced out of the business because of financial reasons.

Faster Change

In the more recent last twenty years or so sources of income in the music business have changed at even a faster rate. We have seen the fall of recording studios due to the rise of home recording studios. We have witnessed the decline in studio gigs for musicians because virtual instruments have become so popular and realistic sounding. We have also seen thousands of songwriters lose their publishing gigs because of the rapid decline of CD (Album) sales, and on and on.

I don't think these types of dramatic changes or shifts in the musical landscape are going to slow down any time soon. This is why it is in the best interest of any person in the music business to *diversify*. Learn another skill or two in addition to your main talent and keep adding to your skill repertoire.

I have witnessed quite a few musicians, artists and songwriters who have figured this out and are now thriving. Let me give you an example.

I know of at least a few guitar players who used to make their living with a combination of live gigging and studio gigs. They still do some of those types of things but as those gigs started drying up they began learning additional skills. They learned basic home recording and engineering skills. They bought themselves a DAW and learned how to get their great guitar to sound wonderful on tape (on their DAW).

They now hire themselves out as guitar players to other producers with home recording studios who need great guitar parts. And they don't just do this in their home town. They record their guitar parts for producers all around the world.

They have taught themselves enough engineering so all a producer has to do is send them a basic song track mp3 file and say "can you give me two or three guitar parts for this song?" They record their guitar track(s), send the WAV files back to the producer and get paid.

They have diversified.

Songwriters

Many songwriters who used to make a decent living from a couple of good album placements per year back in the day when CDs sold millions have now learned enough production, musician and engineering skills to make masters of their songs in their own home recording studios. They are now making at least part of their living licensing those songs to Film and TV shows. They, too, have *diversified*.

I have also witnessed songwriters who used to only write Country Music, now learning and becoming proficient at writing Pop Music and Singer-Songwriter Music. They are *diversifying* within their own skill set and increasing their opportunities and odds for making a better living.

I used to simply write songs for artists but over time I learned how to engineer, produce, and write instrumental "moods" for TV and film. It didn't happen overnight but with a little practice I have become quite good at it. I have *diversified*.

Encouragement

I agree with the principle that to be great, to be the best at any one thing, you probably have to give it most of your time, energy and attention. But I would encourage any musician, songwriter or producer to always be learning additional skills.

If you learn just one new thing every year, in five short years you will have five new skills which can be applied to earning a living.

If you are a bass player (or any other instrumentalist or vocalist), investing in a DAW and spending some time learning how to record your bass parts at home is a brilliant move.

You could also pick up a few students and teach them how to play your instrument and in the process write a book about how to play the bass guitar and then sell your book to a publisher or publish it yourself online.

How about videoing yourself teaching various techniques on your instrument? Then charge a buck a lesson to students around the world. They can pay online or buy it as an app. Who knows, you might get ten-thousand students per month each paying you a buck a lesson. That, indeed, would be bringing home some fresh bacon.

Diversify

For as much as I like it when people spend time getting great at their one thing I don't think in good conscience I would advise anyone to simply do "one thing only" these days.

We live in an ever-changing time when having a diversified skill set is a great and necessary asset to finding continued financial success in the world of music.

More on Diversification in the Music Business

From time to time PROs will shift their royalty rates for one reason or another. This can happen for a variety of reasons including shifts in the economy, new technologies, government intervention, etc.

When these royalty shifts bring me more money – I like it. When they lower the amount I am getting paid – I don't like it at all.

Recently there has been one of these shifts of royalty weighting at some of the PROs. Royalties paid on certain types of music have gone up while royalties paid on other types of music have dropped. These changes have affected me both positively and negatively.

The royalties paid on some of my instrumental cues have slightly risen while the royalties paid on my vocal cues have fizzled.

I tell you this because I want to highlight two important things I have learned in my years of collecting royalties from the PROs.

1. Changes in royalty payment structuring do happen from time to time.
2. There is little to nothing I can personally do that will reverse a negative change.

But there *is* something I can do help protect and buffer me from these inevitable royalty downturns.

Multiple streams of income

As I said in the last chapter, don't put all your eggs in one basket, *diversify*. If for example your sole source of income was from background vocal music in TV shows and you had been making $40,000 per year, a 50% reduction in royalty rate would instantly drop your income to $20,000 annually.

However, if you had the same above amount of music in background TV and you *also* had $10k coming from environmental (Muzak, Mood Media) music and maybe another $8k coming from instrumental TV tracks your annual income drop would be a much lesser percentage.

A decrease, yes, but survivable.

And if you had a few other streams of income coming in (maybe you teach a few students every week and play in a weekend band) your percentage loss would be even less.

Ever Changing

I have weathered these rate reduction storms in music about ten times in the last twenty years mainly because I was diversified. And I continue to diversify seeking new streams of income because history has taught me that there will be rate reduction storms coming again in the future.

I encourage all of my artist friends to continually seek out new and additional sources of income. The storms *will* come and diversification will help you to better survive them.

Below is a list of a few ways to musically diversify and grow your streams of income.

1. First and foremost, write and produce the music you are *good* at creating.

2. Branch out. Write and produce music in different genres.

3. Write instrumentals AND vocal songs (find a collaborator if you only do music or lyrics).

4. Diversify your styles. Write for Film, TV, Environmental Music, Commercials, Artists, Children's Music, Webisodes, Musicals, Smartphones, Video Games, etc...

5. Put your music in multiple libraries and with multiple publishers.

6. Seek out local video and game production companies who might need your music.

7. Seek out local film producers who do not yet have a budget to hire the big guns.

8. Approach your local TV stations and inquire about a music production job.

9. Research and solicit internet companies and advertising agencies.

10. Look for non-traditional ways of marketing your music.

11. Find the most incredible 16 year old singer in the country and offer to produce them... then shop or DIY release the material.

12. Diversify your social media presence. Learn how to use Facebook, Twitter, YouTube, Instagram and whatever the next social media craze is to help you more efficiently market your talents.

13. Package your music as a CD and yourself as an artist. Get your music on iTunes, Spotify, etc...

14. Put your music to videos, upload to Youtube and market through social media. (A couple of great books per marketing yourself through social media are Jay Frank's *Hack Your Hit* and Michael Hyatt's *Platform*.)

15. Play in a band.

16. Teach private music lessons.

17. Write a book or a blog about your experiences (monetize your story).

18. Learn how to engineer and set up a studio business in your home.

These are just a few ways to diversify and keep multiple streams of income coming in.

The weather will change. The storms will come. Build a sturdy shelter.

Diversify.

The Perception of Quality (What is Your Music Worth?)

I have always been a hobby artist.

You know, paintings, drawings and stuff like that.

Even if I was good enough to make a living at it I've never really wanted to try to develop a career selling my oils and acrylics. I always felt like attempting to cash in on my visual creations would ruin the fun of it.

As far back as I can remember, drawing and painting felt special to me. Kind of like making music felt when I was first starting out. Like magic.

Having experienced what can happen to some of that magic when one begins to prostitute their art just to make a buck, which is what I have done with some of my music, I was fairly certain I didn't want to let that happen with my paintings.

I wanted to keep my visual art sacred and enjoyable.

I guess if I *could* have sold my paintings for hundreds of thousands of dollars I would have been into selling them but back in the mid-1990s I couldn't even get a couple hundred bucks for one of my oils.

Until I discovered Rodeo Drive.

Rodeo Drive

My wife and I had taken our children to Disneyland near LA. While we were in that area we decided to take a few extra days and go to the beach and see some of the Southern California sights.

One of the places we ended up spending an afternoon was a place called Rodeo Drive. In case you don't know Rodeo Drive is an upscale, touristy shopping district in Beverly Hills known for its designer fashions and high end boutiques.

It also has a few art galleries sprinkled along its famous three block section. I can't remember the name of the gallery we ended up browsing through but I vividly recall looking at some of the art on display there. It wasn't so much that any particular piece of art caught my attention, it was all fairly average if you ask me, it was the $80,000 price tags that blew my mind.

I remember joking to my wife "if they are getting eighty grand for *this stuff* I should be able to get at least ten grand for my stuff."

Web Sites

A few years later, I think in was 1999, the internet was really starting to take off. Although most people still had slow dial-up web connections many of us had at least gotten a taste of some higher speed internet connections and could see the possibility of where this online thing might go.

I was becoming interested in building web sites and had begun learning html code and even had a couple of web sites up and running. At the same time I was also becoming interested in internet traffic. I found it simply amazing that millions of people could, in just a few short days (hours), discover something new on the internet and all travel there together.

That same year I began getting a little bit of international underground buzz with my jazz music having recently released two CDs – one in '97 and another in early '99.

Perception of Quality

In the winter of 1999 I recall my wife bugging me as she often did to sell some of my visual art. I said to her what I had been saying ever since our Rodeo Drive excursion, "I'm not selling my paintings unless I can get ten thousand dollars for each of them – like those LA people do."

That's when the question first dawned on me, "Why are those artists in the Rodeo Drive art galleries getting eighty-thousand bucks per painting?" Or maybe the better question, "Why are people *paying* eighty thousand dollars for one of those average paintings?"

Rightly or wrongly I reasoned it was mostly due of one thing - *perception*. Or more accurately put - *perception of quality*.

Theory Testing

I wanted to test out my theory. So I began to embark on building a web site and putting pictures of my artwork on it. I only put up eight pieces of what I thought were my best (or goofiest) work on the site. I also put a brief description of me, concocting some story about my journey to become an artist.

I then put prices of the works underneath each photo of my art. But instead of putting a reasonable price of $225 on my paintings, I put the *lowest per-painting* price at $12,000 and the highest at $18,000. I even added a "sold" sign below one of the prices.

Because I had a little buzz about my jazz music at the time I was able to get some eyes on the web site fairly easily. That's when some truly amazing stuff started to happen. Within four weeks I had two magazines interview me and write articles about my art. Within a couple of months, although none of my website artwork had sold, I had two concrete offers to do new paintings. One was for $3000 and the other for $5000.

Wow! My art career was going better than my music career!

Conclusive?

I don't want to say that I am positive I received press attention and high priced (for me) offers because my website presented me as a highly successful artist (which I absolutely was not), but this unscientific evidence sure seemed to clearly point in that direction.

There was a *perception* that if I was good enough to demand fairly high prices then I *was* pretty darn good.

Weird, isn't it?

Advertisers, marketers and corporations have been doing this for years. Telling us that something is great before we have ever even tried it. And we buy into their hype. Often when they list a high price on their goods we automatically *perceive* it as actually being a *better* product.

Conversely, it has often been the case when marketers and corporations *lower* the price on a product or service, it is perceived as being inferior and they actually sell *less*.

To be fair it should be noted that these perception trends are not always the case. Sometimes if you raise the price too high the product doesn't sell at all and if you lower the price on a particular service at the perfect time it will indeed sell more.

Film and TV Music

There is a difference of opinion per the value of music currently swirling around the Film and TV business.

There are many TV shows and Networks that don't want to pay any licensing fee whatsoever to the producers of the music they use in their shows. The only monies collected on the tracks from these shows and networks will come from writing and publishing royalties paid through a PRO.

In the old days this "not paying" thing didn't work because songwriters themselves had to pay for recording studios, engineers, producers and musicians to get their song recorded.

The songwriters could easily have a couple thousand dollars invested in a single song and needed to at the very least make their money back.

Since many of today's songwriters are now producing their own tracks in home recording studios, using virtual instruments and eager to get their music placed on TV shows they are okay with this *backend money only* arrangement. Many are forgoing any production or engineering fees altogether. And it is happening more and more frequently in our business.

This practice leads to the obvious question, "Is this practice of lowering the value of production music going to decrease the amount of money we are making?"

Race to the bottom?

Many are calling this business model of *giving away* music for free a "race to the bottom" – financially speaking. They contend that the *perception* of our music having any value at all is being drastically diminished by this practice.

They also maintain that if everyone attached at least some monetary value to their musical productions (via a licensing fee), then all music will retain its value due to *perception of value* and its perceived equation to quality.

What do you think?

Due to the quality of perception principle I agree with those who maintain that if we do not attach a certain value to our music productions they will soon have little to no value and the practice of giving our product away for free is, indeed, *a race to the bottom.*

Having said that, I also believe there are going to be hundreds if not thousands of writer-producers looking for a break who will continue to give their music away for free for a perceived shot at creating a buzz about themselves.

Supply and demand

My best guess on this issue due to supply and demand is this: There will be many low budget cable shows where music which is used mostly in the background will *not* be paid a licensing fee. Their primary quality quantifier for a track is "does it have the right *mood?*" As long as there are a thousand writer-producers willing to supply them productions for free (or for *backend-only* money) their wallets will be closed.

Yet I also believe there will be many high end TV shows and movies who *do* want their music to be of *quality* in every discernible way. I believe, too, that these folks will continue to be willing to pay substantial licensing fees for the *right* piece of music. At least I hope so.

The perception of quality is indeed a funny thing but a very real thing.

Questions

I won't lie. I have been on both sides of this issue's coin. I have been on the side of not having any placements and willing to do most anything to get on a TV show. I have also been on the other side of the coin watching my licensing fees dwindle down (or go away altogether) in large part because of so many willing to give away their music for free.

I have pretty strong feelings about what I *wish* every writer-producer in the world would collectively do - hold out for at least some money. I also have pretty strong suspicions about what I think many writer-producers *will* do. I think many will give their music away just to get a few placements.

Food for thought: *If music continues to be devalued by people giving it away does the next step of devaluation involve the lowering of, or the elimination of, backend royalties?*

Is it possible that one day performance royalties and mechanical royalties could disappear altogether? What do you think?

Greatest Hits? (In a Music Library)

I have noticed over the last few years a peculiar but pleasing trend happening with some of the instrumental cues I have placed in music libraries. It seems some of them have become my "greatest hits."

Well, maybe I should rephrase or clarify that statement. They have become my greatest hits in the *background TV music biz.*

Much like rock stars have their "hit" songs and their "album cuts" so, too, do we cue writers have our album cuts and our hit tracks.

Radio

Have you ever heard a truly great song by a new artist on your car's radio? What do you do every time that song comes on? If you are like me you probably crank it up and start playing drums on your steering wheel or dashboard.

What else do you do after hearing this cool new song? You probably check out the song's artist to see if they have any other great songs. Sometimes they do and other times the song you heard on the radio is the only good song in their repertoire.

This is one of the reasons we as writers and producers want to have multiple tracks of any particular genre available in each music library we work with and/or in our own personal music library. That way if we have a "hit" track, one a music supervisor falls in love with, that supervisor can seek out and discover our other usable music as well.

Discovery

I have a dramedy track called Mr. Shifty. ("Dramedy," for those who don't know, is comedy flavored music (not too cartoony) often used in dramas that have a comedic flair à la *Desperate Housewives*.) I wrote and recorded Mr. Shifty along with about ten other dramedy tracks a few years ago. They were all signed by a Los Angeles music library. Over these last few years Mr. Shifty has become one of my hits and as of today has been placed over forty times in various TV shows.

It, however, is still a baby hit. Some composers who have been in this game a lot longer than me have had their hit tracks placed *hundreds* of times in TV shows. I'm hoping my baby continues to grow.

One of the great things that can happen when a music supervisor falls in love with one of your tracks is they will often remember *you* – the writer/producer. My track Mr. Shifty not only has the song title (Mr. Shifty) on it, it also has the name *Dean Krippaehne* on the track.

This can be a really good thing. If a music supervisor loves a particular cue in a specific genre with the name Dean Krippaehne on it he or she is very apt to go back to that song's music library to see if there are any other cool cues in the same style by *Dean Krippaehne*.

In Mr. Shifty's case there were an additional ten songs of mine in this LA music library all in that same style and all recorded and ready to go. The music supervisors who liked "Mr. Shifty" discovered them and voila! These songs have also been used on the very same TV shows.

Bad Tracks

Having said that, we must take a look at the other side of this equation.

Have you ever heard a song on the radio that you truly dislike? When you hear that song what do you do? If you are like me you probably immediately change the channel on the radio. Does this irritating song in any way make you to want to go and listen to its artist's other material? Nope. You probably will try to avoid them and their music at all costs.

We need to remember when we sign a cue with a music library or give it to a music supervisor that *our name is attached to it*. For better or for worse it is an advertisement of our composing and production skills. Because our names are listed along with the track's title we want to be very careful not to put any bad compositions or unfinished tracks in any music library.

With some middle-of-the-road music libraries this can easily happen because once our first few tracks have been accepted the library will quite often accept a lot, if not most all of our music.

Note that most of the high-end libraries will not do this. They have higher screening standards and will not let any average work get through. But many of the lower-end, online submission libraries will accept almost anything.

You and I need to be cautious of letting our bad or uncompleted stuff get out there because just as a music supervisor can fall in love with all of our music after hearing one great track, they also can easily steer clear of us because of a couple of bad tracks.

This is something we definitely want to avoid.

We all have tracks that aren't quite working but we often think to ourselves, "Well, in the right situation this track *might* work. I'll put it in a library and see what happens." No! Stop! Don't do this. If you do you will potentially put all of your good music at risk simply because you went ahead and submitted one bad track.

Let it Simmer

Even if you don't know how to fix your average cue and make it sound good right away resist the urge to place it in a library just because you can. Put it on the back burner and listen to it a month from now. After being away from it for a while you will most likely be able to easily identify the track's problem areas and rectify them.

By disciplining ourselves to allow only our best tracks into any music library (or to be heard by any music supervisor) we will always be enhancing our opportunities for placements in Film and TV instead of potentially destroying them.

Lots of songs

It is a good thing to have lots of tracks in music libraries especially when you get a *hit*. But it is never good to have lots of tracks in libraries just for the sake of having lots of tracks.

Your reputation as a writer, producer and artist are at stake.

Yes, give the music libraries lots of songs, but only lots of *really good* songs.

Networking

Networking.

Yuck.

I don't want to do it at all!

Schmoozing around with a bunch of people I don't know.

I'd feel like a phony.

It sounds like absolute torture and I'll look so stupid because I never know what to say!

Introvert/Extrovert

If you are an extrovert you probably light up at the prospect of hanging out with a room full of strangers at a cocktail party. You most likely will jump at any opportunity to get to know new people and share stories and laughter. However, if you are an introvert the mere idea of having to attend that same dreaded cocktail party sounds like pure hell to you. You would be much more comfortable either by yourself or with one or two close friends.

I have heard it said that you can easily tell whether you are an introvert or extrovert by comparing how you feel after a big party with how you feel after hanging out by yourself all day. An extrovert will usually feel invigorated and refreshed after a party even if that party follows a long week of grinding work.

An introvert will usually feel refreshed after some good alone time or time spent with one other friend. The introvert will probably feel absolutely spent and worn out after a big party even if he or she has a good time. The extrovert on the other hand will tend to go bat-crap crazy if he or she has to spend too much time alone without the stimulation of other people.

Swimming

I am an introvert. I am an introvert who has developed extrovert skills. I feel totally refreshed after many hours of alone time and generally tired after spending time with large groups at parties. Don't get me wrong, I *love* people and I especially love being with people now that I have developed some extrovert social skills but I absolutely need my alone time to reboot.

If left to my own devices, if life hadn't pushed me into social situations, I would have probably been a hermit. But my wife is an extrovert and always wants to be around large groups of people. This is how she feels refreshed. So for the sake of our relationship I have had to learn some extrovert people-skills and how to comfortably *hang* at a party.

In the past I have had the good fortune of being forced into a couple of extreme social situations in my work life. During the 1990s I spent ten years playing piano at clubs in Seattle. I needed to socialize with scores of people every night in order to keep my job. In fact, my piano gig demanded that I be the host of the party every night leading others in a good time.

My other major social extrovert gig was being the worship director at a church for over a decade. In my church job I was not only in charge of putting together the music for a couple of worship groups, I needed (and wanted) to have relationships with the many people who were working with me on my music, technical and hospitality teams and I was expected to lead them all (along with the congregation) in prayer multiple times each and every week.

Have you ever had to lead groups of people in prayer? It ain't easy for an introvert. At least not at first.

Talk about trial by fire. In both of those job situations I was in a social party environment six days (and nights) every week - year in and year out. When you are thrown into the water you either learn how to swim or you sink. I learned how to swim. But I am still an introvert by nature.

Music

The importance of networking for the purpose of advancing one's music career cannot be overstated. If you want to build a successful career in five years (instead of twenty-five years) you must network. Networking at music conferences, workshops, seminars, coffee shops and clubs are great places to start developing the relationships needed to open business doors. These are the doors you will need to open if you want to sign deals and make money. Period.

It must be understood, however, that networking is about *relationship building* and not about immediately *selling* your product to a brand new acquaintance.

I find this to be an incredibly freeing reality. When I am just going to a party to hang out, meet a few new people and share some laughs I feel much less pressure than I would if I was taking a CD or a DVD into a party and trying to sell myself.

For these reasons I will never take a CD to networking situations. I do take a business card so if the situation arises, and it often does, I can exchange information with a new acquaintance. Amazingly, over the last many years, I have met people who are now some of my very best new lifelong friends.

Had I never developed the practice of networking I never would have even met these great people who have so enriched my life.

As a wonderful side benefit I have signed about twenty music business deals in the last few years as a direct result from the trust relationships I have made while networking.

It's Too Hard!

Yes, if you are an introvert like me, networking is hard at first. It feels a bit uncomfortable, like getting some golf clubs and learning how to smack that tiny ball down the fairway for the first time. It is clumsy and awkward but rest assured with a little practice, over time, it gets easier and easier.

The best way to start networking is to simply identify a networking opportunity such as a conference or workshop, go there and jump in.

Here is a list of my top 15 networking tips put together from listening to the experts and from my own personal experience.

1. Bring some professional looking, updated business cards. Business cards are really inexpensive. Make some new ones. Keep them simple and to the point.

2. Know your objective. Dig deep and learn who you are and what you have to offer. It is good to write out your goals for each event. Make a plan. Also, don't be everything to everybody. You are *not* everything. If you are best at Punk Rock then state that fact instead of "I do Punk Rock and Reggae and Ambient Drones and Country and Polkas.

3. Write an introduction or an "Elevator Pitch." (A 15 to 20 word summary of yourself that you can speak in 10 seconds.)

4. Elevator Pitch *Part 2*. (If a person is interested have a little more to say about yourself.)

5. Ask questions. People love to talk about themselves and will like you if you let them. Remember that a conversation can be a lot like great music. *Less is more.*

6. Keep your drink in your left hand and don't get tipsy. Keeping your drink in your left hand will keep your handshake hand from getting wet and clammy. Don't get drunk. No matter how fun it may be it is just not professional.

7. Prepare and research. If you are going to a music business party find out who will be there. Research them on the web. That way you can ask them better questions.

8. Be genuine, real and authentic – not fake.

9. Be positive. People are attracted to positive people and repelled by negative people.

10. Be professional. Don't butt in on someone else's conversation. Watch your words and stay with "safe" topics - no politics or religion.

11. Don't talk about your music at first. Ask them about themselves. Get to know them, their likes and needs.

12. Find common ground. I once found out that a music executive loved dogs so we talked about dogs for twenty minutes. I got 20 minutes of a VP's time and became known to him as the cool "dog lover" guy. It laid the foundation for me to build a *relationship* with him.

13. Follow up! Follow up after the event (within one week) with a short "great to meet you" email, social media message or note.

14. Buy stuff. This may sound kind of cheesy but it has worked for me. I have purchased a lot of drinks, coffees, lunches and dinners for potential clients over the years. People love to have stuff bought for them and it gives you great hang time.

15. Repeat all of the above. Again and again.

Fear

Networking is actually incredibly easy. It is really just hanging out with people and having a few laughs. It can, however, be genuinely scary at first for those introverts among us.

My advice to you fellow introverts is to arm yourself with good information and approach the networking event with *no expectations*. Smile, introduce yourself, ask questions, listen and respond. Soon you will begin to get comfortable with the experience and like anything else *the more you do it the better you will become.*

Your fear will begin to subside and your business opportunities will grow. Go for it. You've got nothing to lose and a world of cool relationships to gain.

Generalized Examples of Payment Scales

Example 1: A song on a TV show with 20 million viewers will generally pay more than a song on a TV show with 2 million viewers.

Example 2: A song placed in a TV show's foreground (a song you can hear quite well in the scene) will generally pay more than a song buried behind the scenes dialogue.

Example 3: A song on a radio station with millions of listeners will pay more than a song on a station with hundreds of listeners - at least in theory.

There are many, many other ways songs are weighted. These examples are just a few ways to give you a general idea of how the payment structure works.

I've had cues on network TV pay me in the thousands of dollars per play. I've also had cues on obscure cable networks pay me less than a dollar per play.

Cha Cha Cha Changes

One thing I have noticed over the years is that the PROs will frequently change their *weighting* of songs. ("Weighting" is a term used for discerning monetary value) They usually have a reason these changes although sometimes I do not understand their reasons. (See: Smoke and mirrors)

The Good News

The good news is when you get a cue placed on a TV show or a song released as a single by a recording artist in the USA, as long as you have registered that music with a PRO they will collect any royalties due and cut you a check.

The other good news is if your music is performed overseas, foreign royalties collected by a foreign country's PRO will eventually start trickling in. Or if you have a big hit song those royalties may come flooding in. It can take years for foreign royalties to reach your doorstep but when you start getting payments from countries you have barely heard of it is pretty much coolness.

With TV shows (and in radio plays) these foreign royalties can really add up. Getting multiple song placements in an international hit TV show airing in over 100 countries can bring a good steady flow of income to your mailbox for years.

Also, while there are no movie theater music performance royalties collected in the USA, many other countries pay performance royalties on songs placed in films. These, too, can start to add up as you grow your song placement portfolio.

Take a Licking - Keep on Ticking

There will most likely be some things from time to time that do not go in your favor royalty-wise but you must learn not let it bug you too much. It is just the nature of the beast. Almost every veteran composer and songwriter I know has a horror story of *royalties gone wrong.*

I had my royalties from Muzak (which were substantial) drop by over 60% due to a USA court ruling. My PRO fought the ruling in court but lost. There was nothing much I could do about it unless I wanted to sue the United States of America.

So, there have been bad days but there have been good days as well.

Remember that old watch company ad, *it takes a licking but keeps on ticking?* This pretty much applies to me and needs to apply to anyone who wants to persevere in the music biz. You need to grow a thick skin. I decided to not dwell on what I could not control and to simply put my head down, forge ahead, write some more great music and develop new streams of revenue to help make up for any particular loss in royalty revenue.

That way if they ever rule on the Muzak royalty dispute in my favor I will be doubling my money and dancing on the rooftops.

On the cheerier side of things, sometimes royalties themselves just *keep on ticking* too – and for no apparent reason. Not too long ago I received yet another international royalty check from a single I had with an artist in Japan. It was released way back in 2008. Happy dance!

Summation

I hope this gives you at least some idea of the way performance royalties can work and a few ways they can frustrate you from time to time.

I truly believe that as long as we keep making great music and work on our business network building the royalties will take care of themselves. We only get frustrated when we allow our expectations to get out of whack. And if we are spending too much of our time thinking about the money we may or may not make then we are not spending enough time creating our music and making it what it needs to be.

I find it is always best to not worry about royalties. Just keep making great music.

Now let's get back to work.

Takeaways (Chapters 39 – 49)

1. Technology is changing the way music is delivered and listened to. We need to be aware of new changes so we can best discern how to plan our business models.

2. Cue sheets have been the traditional tracking model for collecting royalties from TV shows.

3. Digital Fingerprinting, in essence, takes a picture of your cue's audio and stores it on servers.

4. Songwriters used to be able to retitle their songs and sign non-exclusive agreements with various publishers thereby enabling themselves to have a single piece of music being shopped by multiple entities.

5. Digital Fingerprinting *may* put an end to retitling. (The jury is still out.)

6. It takes money to make money. We must calculate our risks and invest wisely.

7. To succeed in the music business one must live, eat and breathe relationships, relationships, relationships. (In every aspect and application of the word.)

8. It behooves us to learn how to translate all forms of social and business language. We need to become detectives searching and digging for clues to best decipher what is trying to be communicated to us.

9. The musical landscape is constantly changing. Jobs that exist today may be gone tomorrow.

10. A diversified skill set will increase a creative person's chances for sustained success.

11. Cultivating diversified streams of income will help buffer any adverse musical landscape changes.

12. If you give away your music for free it is possible you are devaluing your music and everyone else's.

13. We benefit from having more than one great cue in any particular genre in a music library. If a music supervisor loves our cue they may come back searching for more.

14. Having subpar music in any library may hinder our chances of securing placements and give us a bad reputation.

15. Networking is relationship building.

16. Relationship building is absolutely imperative to our success in the music business.

17. Relationship building is at its core simply hanging out with other people, having a good time and then staying connected.

18. Networking is just like any other skill. The more you practice it the better you will get.

19. The creator has little control over his or her music royalty rates.

Where did the cheese go?

I recently took a music-biz trip to Nashville.

I love that town.

It is so alive with artists of all kinds.

The sidewalks almost *buzz*.

I have often wondered if Nashville's musician vibe is at all similar to the hum of Paris during the Impressionist art era. Full of life, hope, experimentation, everyone exchanging ideas yet at the same time competing with one another to be noticed.

Cheese

During my week in NashVegas - as the local music biz calls it - one of my many stops was to attend a PMA (Production Music Association) meeting. The PMA is an organization that focuses on trying to keep integrity and value in the production music world. It consists of some of the very top crème of the crop music production companies and libraries.

One of the topics at this particular meeting was, *"are we currently in a race to the bottom?"* This is a hot topic in the production music business world which asks the question, "Are we inadvertently or blatantly devaluing our music by engaging in certain actions and business practices?" And if so, *what can we do to stop this devaluation?*

I touched upon this topic a bit in the *perception of quality* chapter. But I'd like to dig a little deeper since it was the primary issue concerning these Film and TV music pros in Nashville.

The PMA had a panel of production music experts trying to wrestle with this particular issue. One of the comments made by a panelist that struck me with the loudest ring of truth was this: "The cheese has moved." (Using the phrase from Spencer Johnson's popular book *Who Moved My Cheese?*)

That phrase got me thinking. Are we in the music business clinging to an old business model that really doesn't exist anymore? There have been and continue to be a vast number of changes in the music industry due for the most part to the advances in technology and all of its various ramifications. What does this climate of change mean (if anything) to the value of our music?

Different Cheeses

In the last few decades we have seen the proliferation of home computers, the internet, high speed internet, the advent of social media, cell phones and then smart phones. We have also witnessed the video game industry *out earn* the motion picture industry and have seen people go from listening to music on large home speakers to listening to it through the tiny speaker on their iPhone.

In those same last few decades the recording music business has gone from editing music on a two inch tape with a razor blade to "cut and paste" in a DAW. We have gone from the need to hire a live band in our studios to using incredible sounding music software which in many cases has replaced the entire band as well as horn sections and symphony orchestras.

All of these things have had an impact on producing music. I have often said that the same instrumental track I can produce today for *zero* dollars would have cost $2000 to produce in 1990. And one unfortunate consequence of this fact is that at least two thousand dollars has dropped off of the front end fees for our productions.

Cheese whizzes

Also, a musician or a producer no longer needs to be able to play a traditional instrument to create a fabulous production. He or she needs only to have a great ear and know how to *play* a digital studio and virtual software. These days an entire orchestration can be done with one finger playing on a keyboard and that keyboard doesn't have to be a piano keyboard. It can be a computer keyboard.

Because of this a lot more people are now creating music. You no longer need to spend ten years in your bedroom learning how to play your guitar and then five more years honing your chops in the club scene to make great music. You only need a computer, a DAW, some software, an "ear," and a creative curiosity to become a rock star.

Yeah, stuff has changed. The cheese has moved.

So Many Cheeses

I do not want the value of music to go down but maybe in a way it already has.

Just a few short decades ago our main forms of technology-type home entertainment were watching TV (just a few channels), listening to the radio and enjoying our records on a stereo system. These were the three major choices and two of them were music focused.

Because it was one of only a few home entertainment choices, thirty five years ago recorded music had an extremely high value.

Today we have many more home technology entertainment choices. Our everyday choices include traditional TV, hundreds of cable channels, On Demand, Netflix, Youtube, Hulu, social media, Google, online games, cell phones, smart phones, texting, Facebook, Twitter, Snapchat, Instagram, Pinterest, hourly news and sports online, our home stereo, radio, Wii games, iPads, a trillion other apps and new choices every day.

Music is no longer the *two-thirds* of our home entertainment choices it once was. It is about *one one-hundredth* or less of our entertainment choices.

As a form of entertainment music has been devalued by virtue of so many other entertainment options becoming a reality in our lives. It does not matter whether I like this new reality or not. It is what it is. There is more competition for people's eyes and ears than ever before. The cheese is moving.

Think about it. When the covered wagon was our primary means of transportation it had great value. When you add a car, a train, a motorcycle and a jet airplane to the mix the covered wagon is far less valuable. It still may be the coolest covered wagon on the block but if people would rather drive a car, well...

A Cheesy Analogy

Before you get too mad at me for suggesting that music may have less value than it once did let me assure you that at least in one way music has the same value it always did. Hundreds of years ago the vast majority of people in Europe attended church on a regular basis. Today only a small percentage of people in most of Europe attend church regularly.

So, has God lost His value? Absolutely not. God has the exact same value God has always had and will always have. (Atheists ignore this part.) But, indeed, "churches" have lost some value at least *in the minds of the consumer*.

Apples

Here's another way to look at it.

Once upon a time there were three apple growers who grew three kinds of apples. It was the only fruit in town. All three apples tasted equally great so all three apple growers got together and decided to price them equally. The agreed upon price was one dollar per apple.

Although that price seemed kind of high to many people the apples were so delicious that people bought them and enjoyed them.

Years went by until one day people began to discover that anyone could get a piece of land and grow apples. Soon after this discovery there were five hundred apple growers. Many of these grower's apples were not great tasting but they still tasted good enough.

They - the *new* apple growers - decided that in order to compete with the original three great apple growers they would have to price their apples much lower. So they priced them at ten cents per apple.

People liked the new lower prices of the apples and after trying them they discovered that although the apples weren't great they were pretty good and surely edible.

The three great apple growers were furious. "All apples are worth one dollar!" they adamantly exclaimed. They even formed an apple club and convinced ten other apple growers to price their apples at one dollar per apple.

But there was a problem.

One hundred of the new apple growers were keeping their price at ten cents per apple no matter what. Soon people weren't buying many of the "dollar" apples anymore. There was also an additional problem for the three great apple growers. There were new farmers who had discovered new types of fruits and were now growing oranges, bananas and mangos. AND they were selling them for ten cents a whack!

Fewer and fewer people were paying one dollar for the apples grown by the three great apple growers. They now had a choice to make. They needed a new business plan. They either had to lower their apple price or think of some new way to keep their revenue stream flowing if they wanted to stay in business.

Two of the great apple growers did not lower their prices nor did they try anything new. They soon failed and went out of business. One of the great apple growers, however, began to thrive. What did he do? He lowered the price of his great apple to 50 cents finding that some people would still pay that amount for the best tasting apple in town. He also started growing the other fruits and grew the best tasting ones of all.

And he did a third amazing thing. He discovered vegetables. No one else in town knew about these crazy vegetables. He was the only grower. He sold carrots for a buck apiece. People loved these new carrots and bought them at full price.

The last great apple grower was very happy.

Do you get the picture?

Still Cheese on the Shelf

The good news for us producers of music is where there were only three or four media venues that used to use our material a few short decades ago, today there are scores of media venues wanting to use our music and the number of new venues keeps growing.

And - AND - there are many undiscovered venues and music products waiting for us to seize and offer to the masses.

I do not know where the cheese has been moved to but my best guess is the value of music (the amount we are paid from a particular venue) may continue to decrease. Again, I don't like this. But I also think a piece of music that used to pay us royalties from two or three venues may - in the future - pay us from twenty or thirty or three-hundred media venues. Just smaller amounts from each venue.

Cheese Heads

I hope I am wrong. I hope the monetary value of music either stays the same or increases. I hope what once paid me two thousand dollars will in the future pay me four thousand dollars. I hope. I hope.

But sitting there in Nashville at that PMA meeting listening to various panelists make their case my gut told me something different. It said something with the ring of truth to it. Something I didn't want to hear but *needed* to hear.

The cheese has moved.

Get Your Brand New Space-age iPhone Transistor Radio

The other day my daughter and one of her friends wanted me to check out a new teen song they were raving about. My daughter pulled out her iPhone and proceeded to press play. The drums and claps kicked in and the chorus began its hypnotic rhythm. Both of the girls giggled, danced and sang along with this new song's catchy hook line.

This same scene has repeated itself a number of times in my life these last few years. Friends have been pulling out their Android or iPhone devices and pointing them toward my ears so I can hear and experience the latest greatest song they have discovered.

Just this morning while having coffee with a friend he made a few finger pushes on his iPhone, stuck it in my face and said "dude, you gotta watch this." I must confess the video he wanted me to see was truly impressive but the sound coming through the iPhone speakers was....uh... not so impressive. (Putting it kindly.)

He didn't seem to mind. Neither did the giggling girls I just told you about.

That wonderful emotional buzz so many of us used to get from sitting in front of a gigantic wall of Altec Lansing speakers blaring out the latest James Taylor or Blue Oyster Cult record is for the most part a fading piece of boomer lore. Most of the new generations and even the older generations are now listening to much of their music on tiny sub-par (in my opinion) Droid or iPhone speakers. *And they are perfectly okay with it.*

Crazy

When I was a kid I had this cool thing. It was called a *transistor radio*. It was the dawning of the space age and listening to a radio you could hold in the palm of your hand was, well... groovy. This new transistor radio was about the size of an iPhone only much thicker. I loved this crazy gadget. It enabled me to tune in to my favorite Rock n Roll radio station and hear my favorite new songs anytime day or night. This tiny radio became like an additional appendage, a part of my body and being - my swag.

I will say, however, that the sound of my transistor radio, well, sucked.

One of the coolest things to happen to me in my young life was making enough money to buy my first stereo system. It had these BIG, wonderful, awesome speakers. And after I purchased it I had just enough money left over to buy a couple of new albums. (If you don't know what an *album* is go backwards through time with me: Spotify - iTunes - Mp3 - CD - Cassette - Eight-Track Tape - Albums) I then put one of my new vinyl albums on the turntable and sat in pure bliss as I listened to the music which had an amazingly BIG *sonic sound* coming through these incredible new speakers of mine. It was heaven.

On the other hand my transistor radio's sound was terrible. Sure it was a handy and affordable device but its tinny sounding speakers left much to be desired. My stereo's sound, as expensive as it was, was worth every penny.

Do people even have stereo systems with great speakers anymore?

Of course some people these days do have big stereo systems but the trend of the last many years is one of people listening to their music more and more through less and less. What is hip today is listening to your jams through what I would call sub-par speakers.

These sub-par systems include our iPhones, Droids, laptops, pads and also our desktop's cheesy sounding systems.

As I sat there watching my daughter and her friend fully enjoying the song coming through the tinny sounding speakers I had to ask myself if the way these new generations are listening to music will affect the way in which we *write our songs* and *produce our music*.

Interesting question isn't it. Will new technologies change the way in which we approach making music?

Piano Rolls

New music guru and author Jay Frank in his brilliant book *FutureHit.dna* makes the argument that technology has always influenced if not *driven* the changes in music composition and production. (I recommend checking out his books when you get a chance. He makes compelling cases using historical facts and modern day statistical analysis.)

One of the things that intrigued me in Jay Frank's research was how the three minute standard-length pop song came to be. Evidently, when player-pianos became popular over 100 years ago the *piano rolls* used to play the music inside of these pianos would only hold about three minutes worth of paper and no more.

For songwriters to sell their wares they had to adapt to this new piano roll technology and write songs that were no longer than three minutes. Bam! That was the real reason for and the beginning of the 3-minute song becoming a pop-culture standard. I know, right?

Also, back in the old-school car-radio days you had to work quite hard to tune your car's radio dial to find your favorite station. Changing from one station to another involved turning the dial again and then carefully and meticulously getting your dial to find the *sweet spot* where there was no static. It was doable but not easy. So consequently when you finally got your favorite station tuned in you were fairly likely to stay there due to the frustrating trouble of changing channels and trying to tune-in to another station.

Yet when digital radio came along changing from station to station was automatic. Just a quick push of the button and you were there. This was a wonderful innovation for users but a nightmare for some radio programmers because you could now so very easily leave their station and click over to some rival station.

As a result songwriters and producers were pushed to have shorter and shorter intros to their songs so you didn't bore the listener causing them to click away. Songwriters also had to get to the chorus faster (again, so you didn't lose the listener) and write their song's *verses* with some kind of "hook" so as not to have the listener simply push his digital radio button and go elsewhere because they got too bored with a non-hooky verse.

If you analyze the hit Pop songs of today with the hit songs of twenty-five years ago you will notice a profound difference. Today's current songs have shorter intros (or no intro), hookier verses and they all get to the chorus much, much quicker than did the songs of the 70s and 80s.

It appears that once again over the last twenty to thirty years technology may have indeed *driven* the evolution in songwriting and production styles. Freaky, isn't it?

Back to the iPhone and the Android...

As I sat there watching my daughter and her friend dancing away to their new favorite song on their smart phone it dawned on me that certain types of songs and productions will work quite well in these *new tinny speakers* and other styles will not work so well.

On smart phone speakers you can plainly hear the kick and snare drum with their simple straight-ahead and danceable beat churning out the groove. You can also hear quite plainly the lead vocal spanking out its rhythmic, melodic hook and making you want to bob your head and sing along with the singer's cadence.

It was amazing to me that, with the exception of a stark guitar or synthesizer riff here and there, these were about the only production attributes you could hear on my daughter's tiny iPhone speakers. And even more amazing to me was the fact that this substandard sonic quality was of no concern to those two giggling girls - whatsoever!

So I am wondering what effect, if any, this new way of "listening" to music will have on the way we might create it?

I would imagine that a lush sound or ethereal music would not work well on smart phone speakers and a Joni Mitchell ballad from her iconic album *Blue* might have very little impact presented in this miniature music forum. Songs too complicated in rhythm and texture or too esoteric in style might not "cut through" or translate well on tinny sounding speakers either.

What then will translate well on the listening devices of today like the iPhone and Droid?
That question begs this question: What worked well on the transistor radios of the 60s?
One thing that always worked quite well on those old transistors was *bubblegum pop*.

Yup! Songs with straight-ahead, relatively simple beats and catchy choruses elementary enough to sing along with but rhythmic enough not to get lost in all the "tin" and plastic. Those types of songs will work quite well.

Are we going back to the day and age of the single, the one hit wonder and the disposable bubblegum-pop of yesteryear? Maybe - maybe not. Or maybe we have never left. I like bubblegum Pop so I'm cool with it becoming a modern day radio staple but I also enjoy a variety of other song styles.

The good news for all of you bubblegum haters is that even during that 60s era of bubblegum-friendly transistor radios some other types of incredible music was being made and also sounded *just good enough* on those vintage hand held devices to move and groove us.

Have hope.

Here There and Everywhere

I finally got around to reading Geoff Emerick's brilliant book *Here, There and Everywhere* about his life as recording engineer for The Beatles.

Geoff was the primary recording engineer for the Beatles throughout most of the mid-60s until the band's ultimate demise.

His book recounts numerous insider stories never before told about the band.

He also gives great insight to how he, producer George Martin and the Beatles discovered many new recording techniques in what was quite possibly the most inventive and innovative era in modern music.

Every few pages seem to unveil yet another musical gem to ponder and analyze. Here are a couple of those gems.

Ringo's Drums

Back in the old sterile corporate days of recording when engineers wore white coats, dress shirts and black ties to work looking much more like research scientists than hip-music-dudes, EMI (the gigantic record company) had a rule about its microphones.

It was strictly stated that no mic was ever to be placed closer than two feet from the drums. Breaking this policy was grounds for immediate dismissal from the company.

Recording engineer Geoff Emerick, unhappy with the sound of Ringo's drums on the song "Tomorrow Never Knows" (from the *Revolver* album), decided for the sake of a possible better drum sound he would risk being fired and venture moving the drum mics past the dreaded two foot zone. He then proceeded to move each mic just a few *inches* from the drum heads. (Gasp!)

This may have been the first time (certainly one of first times) a drum kit had ever been close-miked. (Close-miking the drums is a technique that has now been commonplace for decades.) After he had done this risky move with the microphones he found someone's discarded wool sweater, removed the bass drum head and shoved the sweater inside up against the beater-skin to dampen the sound. (What?!)

Again, this *dampening of the drums* is a commonly used procedure these days to get a tighter drum sound but back then it was all experimentation and innovation. No one knew what the result would be.

As soon as the band did another take of the song and listened back to the results they were all blown away by this new drum sound coming out of the speakers. Never before had they heard such tight, punchy drums. Everyone was exuberant because the results of this microphone *violation* brought even more excitement and life to the sound of an already energetic band.

They were all sold on Geoff as an engineer and on the idea of experimentation. And long before the phrase *thinking outside the box* was coined they were living and breathing it.

Pay it Forward

This studio experimentation and discovery process which was so much a part of the late 60s Beatles era causes me to ask a couple questions of myself - and of you. Are we doing any experimenting in our writing and recording? What new recording techniques have we discovered lately?

There is always something new to discover. There is always a new way to get a cool, unique sound. Have you discovered anything lately? If so, I urge you to share it with someone. Pay it forward - so to speak.

Many of the cool techniques I use to make my music productions sound better have been learned from other artists *paying it forward*. For example, I've learned that sometimes a real effective way to get a modern-day Pop snare sound is by combining three of four different snare sound samples.

Quite often this process of combining multiple snare or percussion sounds will give me something that resonates in a variety of frequencies bringing a new "bigness" and massive punch to the snare sound.

I've also learned that if your Pop song's snare drum is hitting on 2 and 4 it can be quite interesting to stack an additional subtle snare or percussive sound on the "4" of every measure. This slight difference in sound between the snare hits on 2 and 4 gives the snare drum and song even more interest and helps to hold the listener's ear without being too obvious about it.

How did I learn this? *Someone told me.* This was *their* process. They paid it forward.

I have learned too, that if you have a great viola sound but it needs to be a tad warmer or a bit softer, you can add a unison French Horn line to your viola line and with the proper mix, magic happens. Your viola still cuts through the track but in a softer and more delicate way. This can be extremely helpful in a tender ballad where you desire a counterpoint viola part but don't want the instrument to jump out and bite the listener's ear.

Yes, someone shared this trick with me as well.

I love experimenting with lyrics in songs. Recently I was getting tired of hearing the same old rhyming schemes over and over again in my songs (and in the hit songs on the radio). A songwriting friend suggested I try something radical. He said "don't rhyme." He suggested I rhyme the first couple of lines to set the listener's ear up to expect another sequential rhyme but then at the next expected rhyming place - don't do it - don't rhyme.

As soon as I tried this trick I almost fell out of my chair in utter amazement. Suddenly my new non-rhyming lyric sounded hip, fresh and new. My whole song sounded hip and new. It was incredibly exciting. I don't think I would have ever thought of doing this all on my own.

The point here is to experiment. To try something new in your songs and productions and if it sounds cool - pass it on. Share it with someone. *Pay it forward*. Let's keep this creativity thing rolling.

New Technology

Another thing I thought was a good lesson in Geoff Emerick's book was when he was talking about mixing the *Revolver* and *Sgt. Pepper's* albums in *mono*. He maintains the mono mixes of these two records are far superior to the stereo mixes because weeks were spent mixing these records in mono and only *a few days* were spent doing stereo mixes.

Evidently, the Beatles thought the new stereo thing was just a passing fad. They thought it would never catch on. That's why they didn't spend much time on those mixes.

I found it wonderfully delightful that some of the most creative minds of our time working on one of the most highly revered albums of our time (Sgt. Peppers) completely missed the significance of a brand new technology – stereo recording. I love this because it is documentation that the Beatles were human too.

It made me wonder what new technology is right in front of our noses that we are for whatever reason missing or dismissing. I have friends who told me twenty years ago that computer recording would never replace what they thought was the real thing - tape. Oops, they were wrong.

Food

I just read about a guy who is inventing a 3-D printer he hopes will one day print food. Yes, *food!* Entire meals for you and I to feast upon right in our very home all made by a 3-D printer. "I'll have a carrot and some fried chicken." His idea is one day we will simply hit a few buttons and five minutes later our dinner will be *printed up* and served.

Nah. It'll never work.

And stereo will never catch on.

Takeaways (Chapters 50 – 52)

1. Music used to be one of just a few home entertainment options.

2. Today there are hundreds (or more) non-music based media entertainment options in our homes.

3. Has music been devalued due to onslaught of media entertainment options?

4. Will we discover new and unique ways to monetize music?

5. Technology has changed the way we listen to music.

6. Technology has always influenced the way music is created.

7. Retain the joy of discovery in your music. Experiment.

8. If you discover something new, pay it forward.

Do These Songs Make My Music Look Phat?

I like to run.

Well, I call it running.

Most people would call what I do jogging.

I am real slow.

Sometimes elderly people using walkers pass me by.

But saying I am a *runner* makes me feel more like an athlete.

My philosophy is quite simple, "if I am putting one foot in front of the other and it is faster than a walk, I am not jogging - I am *running*."

Ouch

Not too long ago I was out on a late April afternoon run. It had been raining earlier in the day but the pavement was fairly dry. I remember coming up to a corner where I had to take a right turn onto a new street. It was a residential area in the suburbs and there was this majestic house on the corner's lot that had a beautiful, magnificent, sprawling front lawn.

It was a massive green blanket that my brand new running shoes were yearning to float across. Without giving it a second thought I jumped the curb, forded the sidewalk and landed one foot squarely on the edge of this terraced, green wonderland.

If I had taken the time to contemplate my actions I quite possibly would have decided against putting the full weight of my body-in-motion on this damp, emerald landscape. You see I had failed to calculate that the moisture from the morning's precipitation was still clinging to those thousands of grass blades which were now supposed to be the foundation of my stability.

They say life can turn on a dime and this is true.

It is also true that when a runner hits wet grass in full stride his body can fall on its…well, arse. I hit the ground hard. *Real* hard. With an un-acrobatic thud. Bam! "Man down!"

The most amazing thing about my fall was not the fall itself. It only lasted maybe two seconds. Much more incredible was the superhero-like quickness I used to instantaneously get back on my feet again. Never before in my entire life have I moved with such blinding speed than I did rebooting myself from that awkward moment on my bum.

However, I did not immediately check to see how badly I was hurt. The very first thing I did after putting on my circus-like performance was to quickly look around to see if anyone had seen my embarrassing dorkyness.

Yes, I am like that. Totally self-centered, absolutely vain and overly concerned with how my actions may look to others in any given moment. I know this is not a flattering attribute but it is nevertheless part of who I am. To this day I am still regretfully very much concerned with whether or not people view me as the complete idiot or if I can continue to *fake them out*. Sigh.

The Coin's Flipside

I must say though that this overly-concerned nature of mine has at least served me somewhat well in my music productions and songwriting.

When I am writing, when I am creating, I am usually in my own little world unconcerned with what others may think. I am simply free to go wherever the muse leads which is probably the only way one can be truly creative. But at some point in my process I need to switch over to *editor mode* and try to imagine how *others* will hear or view whatever it is I am attempting to create.

The reason for this is simple. I want to make money on my creations. And having a sense of how others will view my work can enhance my chances of financial success.

(Note: If you are purely creating for artistic purposes without any intention of ever making a dime then what I am writing here does not apply to you. You can stop reading. And I bow down and applaud you for your artistic purity. It is indeed admirable. I am not that kind of a purist. I want to buy a new car.)

From a business standpoint it does not matter if I think I have created the greatest song in the history of mankind. From a business standpoint what matters most is whether *others* think my song is great or not. They are the ones who will potentially buy and sell my music so *their* connection with it is, indeed, of the utmost importance.

I have had the good fortune over the years of being in situations where I've been able to test my material on live audiences and gauge their response. I always do this mindfully and honestly looking for signs of audience connection such as: Did they stop their conversations and pay attention to the song? Did the music cause them to immediately want to get up and dance or move in some way? Did the song fall flat with no one paying any attention to it in any way whatsoever?

These are important clues to whether or not I am hitting my mark and connecting with an audience.

Take it for a Test Drive

I would encourage any writer or producer to get out and perform their music before a live audience and try to gauge the crowd response for the purpose of measuring its *connectivity*. If you are not a performer I would urge you to find a local performer or band and persuade them to perform your music in front of a live audience so that you can scan the people as your song is being played. If you want to know how well your music machine runs you've got to take it for a test drive.

Sure, you must take into account whether or not the *performance* helps or hurts your material. But you should be able to get some idea if it is hitting or missing the mark by weighing all of the factors.

Maybe there is a local DJ in your community you can befriend. And maybe you can convince him or her to spin your track in a Friday night club. Are people groovin' to it? (Is the word *groovin'* even used anymore?)

If you cannot do any of the above there is still hope, don't despair. In these days of home recording studios, smart phones and flip-cams it is relatively easy to make a video production of your music and test drive it on YouTube, Facebook or some other form of social media where you can gauge its connectivity with real live (online) people.

Via social media you can find out almost instantly if your production has a super connection or not. If your video only gets 300 views or listens in a month it is probably not connecting very well. Why? Because if those 300 listeners had truly *loved* your song they would have shared it with everyone and your three hundred hits would have become 300,000 or three million almost overnight.

We live in a very unique time. If your song/video creation *truly* connects with people you will know it immediately. This, however, does not mean your music is good or bad it just means that something about your creation *connected*. We have all seen hideous performances get millions of views in one week. This is often because the performance is so humorously awful everyone wants to share it with their friends. But as bad as it might have been, it - the terrible performance - *connected*.

Beware

The first people we usually want to play our music for are our family and friends. This is ok as long as we remember that family and friends tend to want to support us and because of that fact they will not always give the most *honest* opinion about our songs. We need to make sure we also play our music for people who are not family and friends as they will give us a much more objective response.

Your mother will probably love each one of your new songs and will want you to play them in front of all of her friends because she loves you and wants to show you off. This is nice but it is doubtful her opinion has any useful objectivity whatsoever. But playing your songs for a room full of strangers who could care less about you will indeed give you some objectivity about the potential marketability of your music.

I also know from personal experience that playing your Country song for a guy who listens mostly to Metal is not the best gauge of its viability in the Country market. He most likely will not like it. Not because it is a bad song but because he doesn't listen to or like Country music. (I know I'm stereotyping. Lots of Metal people love Country music.) The vice versa thing applies here too as do any other polarizing genre comparisons.

If you are a Pop music person get Pop music people to hear your stuff and if you are a jazz cat, get other jazz folks to check out your hipness.

Paying close attention to how people respond to our music and the music of others will give us valuable insight on what kinds of things people respond to and suggest to us adjustments we may need to make for our music to better connect with an audience.

Rejection (Learning to Deal with Disappointment)

So your music was rejected.

The big "R."

Again.

Congratulations!

You are doing something right.

By submitting your music you are allowing it to be scrutinized by others which is a huge step beyond what most people will do.

Everyone

I wanted to address rejection in the music biz because virtually everyone I know who is successful - *everyone* - has had their material rejected hundreds of times. It is simply part of the business. In a way it is probably the biggest part of the entertainment business.

Everyone will have to learn to deal with dozens of "no's" to get to one "yes." You may get lucky and get a 'yes' early in the game but you will earn it with many "no's" later on - trust me.

You may even get on a roll and have a few hit songs and hear nothing but "yes" for a while but sooner or later you will board the *no train* once again.

Remember though you are in good company. Even the Beatles and Elvis heard no before they heard yes.

Ouch Again

It has been said that the most important attribute a person can have in this business is perseverance. Have you ever wondered why successful music business people say that? They say it at least in part because of one word: *rejection*. They know what it feels like. They have been there unable to sleep at night wondering if they will ever get that one *break*.

They have slogged through months and years of frustration and somehow managed to kick the dirt off their boots, get back in the muck and keep walking forward. You need to be able to grow the skill of persevering through resistance and overcoming rejection if you want to have the success you so desire.

Having said that I will commiserate with you for just a moment or two. Rejection stings. I just had two of my songs rejected a few days ago. I didn't like it. I felt a little twang in my gut, mumbled a few words my mother wouldn't like and then moved on.

Let me ask you a question.

How did you react the last time your work was rejected? Did you rant and rave while you were all alone in your apartment? That's okay. Did you call the person who rejected your stuff and scream at them or post mean things about them online? I hope not. That is *not* okay. I've seen it happen before. Blasting someone who rejected your art is unprofessional and will quickly give you a reputation you do not want to have.

Losing your cool even one time to a business professional can cost you tons of work and music making opportunities.

Each project manager who you submit your music to is usually looking for something specific or they are looking to *feel that magic* in what they hear. This personal *feeling* is often highly subjective and unique to them. In other words, you have absolutely no control over how they will respond to your music – none – so *let it go*.

If you have been turned down and can't let go you will only beat yourself up and cause yourself grief and pain by holding on to your negative emotional reaction. Whether someone likes your music or not is something totally out of your ability to control or influence.

I find it best to just give myself a six-second tantrum and then move on. Don't think about it anymore. Get busy on a new project. The only thing you or I have control over is our work. We have absolutely no control over someone's response to it.

Let me say it again. *We have no control over someone's response to our music. If they don't like it - let it go and move on.*

The R Word

Let's dig a little deeper for a moment into our own personal psychological state of being.

Be absolutely honest with yourself.

How do you react when rejection comes knocking at your door?

Do you just naturally say "oh well, *c'est la vie*" and then get on with something new?

Or do you let negative thoughts roll around in your head becoming bigger and bigger, igniting more negative thoughts and feelings which snowball into a cascade of frustration, dejection and depression. Have you ever let those feelings lead to weeks and weeks where you are unable to create anything new whatsoever?

If so I've got a tip for you.

Don't let your thoughts go there. *When you control your thoughts you will control the way you feel.* If you let your thoughts run rampant they will be controlling your emotional state.

In other words, *if you don't learn to control your thinking you will be a prisoner to your own thoughts.* This is Psychology 101 through PhD.

Truth

Learn to tell yourself the truth. An example: *"My stuff was rejected. I don't like it but it's okay. It is not horrible to be rejected and I can still have a great life and create more cool stuff even if my art sometimes doesn't get accepted. Being rejected is unpleasant but there will always be hundreds of opportunities to submit my work elsewhere."*

Don't buy into the lies of distorted thinking or *cognitive distortions* as psychologists would call it. Lies like this: *"I hate the person that turned down my stuff, they suck. I'll never get another chance as good as this one. Being turned down is horrible and terrible. Maybe I really am no good. I feel sick. Screw everybody, nobody gets me and what I do. I hate my life."*

This is distorted thinking.

Believe it or not, many people process life's events with this kind of distorted thinking. I once did. I don't anymore. It is terribly destructive to let your distorted thought process dictate your life.

Forward Motion

One way to deal with rejection is to just keep moving forward. The two songs of mine that were rejected a few days ago had already been cut, placed and have made me nearly forty-thousand-buckaroonies between the two of them on other projects. I *know* that these songs are good - for the right project. Obviously, because they were turned down this time the person in charge of this particular project didn't think they were a good fit. And he may be 100% correct in his assessment - or 100% wrong. It doesn't matter. He gets to decide. Not me.

He is in charge, he is in control, he gets to make the decision and guess what? My songs are out.

So I gave myself six seconds of *boohoo* and then I *let it go*. I am now already recording and submitting new music to new projects.

Critiques

Another way to deal with rejection is to *use* it. Find out the reason or reasons why someone passed on your work. Sometimes we can find out this information and sometimes we cannot. If we are lucky enough to get feedback from our rejecters we can often learn from it and apply the lessons to our next work or our next pitches.

I once had some really cool piano jazz music turned down for a TV placement. And then it was turned down again - and again. I was able to talk to one of the people who rejected it and discovered that although they thought my piano jazz piece was cool, there were too many notes playing too fast for it to sit comfortably underneath the dialogue of a TV actor. So even though it was a good piece of music, in a TV situation it distracted from the scene instead of adding to the scene's vibe.

Cool. I learned something. And as I started writing new piano jazz pieces for TV I gave those cues fewer crazy notes. It took a bit of time and practice but I learned to give my songs space. I let them breathe which in turn gave the actor's dialogue room to move and let the scenes breathe. And I did all of this because one person who had rejected my piano jazz told me something – *and I listened*.

Sometimes we can learn from rejection and sometimes we just have to let it be.

If you have recently been rejected and are having trouble controlling your negative thought process I would suggest you do whatever it takes to dig in and start working on something new.

One of the best forms of therapy to help silence the out-of-control type of thinking we sometimes experience is *distraction* and one of the best ways to distract our minds is to occupy them with the thoughts of our new work.

Rejection

No one likes rejection but if we are putting our talents out there in the greater entertainment business we must learn to deal with it. Rejection is, in a way, the biggest part of this business

Isn't This Supposed to be Fun?

Have you ever felt like making music has become a chore?

I know I have felt that way sometimes.

Much of my advice to fellow artists actually centers on helping them to get serious about growing their music business skills. But getting serious doesn't mean creating music and having a good business head should lead to days filled with drudgery.

I think the main reason I focus so much on the discipline of craft and actually doing our work is because discipline and work ethic are often the only things standing in the way of us artist types making a living.

However, there is another aspect to creating music we must not forget.

Are you ready? Drum roll...

Making music is supposed to be fun.

Rumours

I have recently been reading a couple of books that have caused me to rethink my creative process. The first is a book I want to tell you about is called *Making Rumours*. It is an inside story written by producer-engineer Ken Caillat about the making of Fleetwood Mac's classic album *Rumours*.

In this book (which by the way I enjoyed tremendously), Ken Caillat recounts numerous stories about the writing, recording and the experimentation involved in creating Fleetwood Mac's masterpiece. He talks about trying to get the best sound out of each instrument and the greatest performance out of each player. He gives us a bird's eye view to the collective discovery of this band's exciting new sounds at what was quite possibly the apex of their innovation.

He also elaborates on each musician's process of trial and error in trying to bring their best artistry to each and every song. There are quite a few times when Ken Caillat mentions the joy of *cranking up the speakers to ten* and listening to the music with a little buzz on.

It becomes quite clear that all involved in the project are making music for the pure joy of discovery, experience and to seek to create something that is cool. And although most everyone who was a part of making of Fleetwood Mac's *Rumours* album eventually made tremendous amounts of money it is apparent through the author's stories that none were at the time creating music with *making money* in mind.

They were seeking *flow*. They were searching for that *feeling*. They were *having fun*.

Those were their glory days.

Intrinsic

Another fascinating book I have recently read is called *Drive* written by Daniel H. Pink. This book is largely about what *motivates* an individual. In this book Daniel H. Pink gives us a wealth of information and cites countless studies all of which overwhelmingly conclude that what motivates us is not what we think it is nor is it what we have been taught.

Most of us think and have been taught that what motivates us to achieve a goal or complete a task is extrinsic. Extrinsic meaning a reward or a carrot dangled out in front of us. Something we will chase after, such as a higher salary or a big promotion or fame and fortune.

Study after study has not only proven this to be wrong in creative endeavors but has clearly shown extrinsic motivation to run counter to productivity. When someone's primary motivation is extrinsic and they are given a promotion or a raise in pay they will actually perform *worse* than if no promotion or additional monies were given at all.

These studies primarily apply to the creative problem solving types of work. If a person's job is algorithmic in nature - meaning they simply follow a step by step procedure to reach a goal - extrinsic motivators are of no hindrance to performance.

What is overwhelmingly shown again and again in these studies is when we are performing our creative problem solving for *intrinsic* reasons (i.e. internal motivations such as joy and personal satisfaction) both quality and productivity go up. Way up!

Amazingly when the subjects in all of these studies were given problem solving activities and promised no extrinsic rewards at all they *always* did better. Unencumbered by extrinsic "carrots," they were able to tap into the intrinsic joy of discovery and challenge.

For the Love

In other words when you and I are being creative - if we love what we are doing - we will have fun doing it. And studies have conclusively shown that this fun and joy we experience will translate into a better product.

I will probably continue to preach discipline and work ethic primarily because so many creative types are lacking in those areas and need to be reminded to actually *do* their work instead of simply *dreaming* about it.

But I think, too, that those of us who are being diligent in our work process need to remind ourselves every now and then that making music is supposed to be *fun*.

So crack open a cold one, crank up the volume and rock out.

Something very cool will most likely come of it.

Can One Small Change Make a Big Difference?

We have already addressed how one small change can make a big difference in our songwriting and music productions (see: Chapter 30 "Free Falling"). But how about in our business dealings or in our lives? Can changing one thing in our life really make a big difference? Can changing one tiny aspect of the way we run our business increase bottom line revenue?

Cabbies

In New York City a taxi cab driver makes around $90,000 in gross annual revenue. There are somewhere around thirteen-thousand taxi cab drivers in NYC.

Up until the year 2007 a cabbie's decision of whether or not to accept credit cards was voluntary. In 2007 New York City made it mandatory for all taxis to take credit cards.

Most installed a touch screen payment machine which had only three button choices for tipping. Those choices were for the amounts of 20%, 25% and 30%.

Before 2007 when many of the taxi transactions were cash the average tip was 10%. After the installation of the credit card machines the average tip rate rose to 22%.

This *one small change* of installing credit card machines with only three tipping options resulted in an annual increase of $140,000,000 for taxi drivers.

Wow!

So let me ask the question again. *Can one small change make a big difference?*

Game Changers

What is one thing in your day to day life you could change or do that could potentially make a big difference? Here are three *personal* changes I have made in the past that have had a profound impact on the quality of my life:

* *Exercising daily.* Daily exercise has led me to being healthy and fit and I feel good most *all* of the time.

* *Healthy diet.* Eating healthy food has led to both weight management and consistent high levels of daily energy.

* *Reading positive authors.* This daily habit has filled my mind with "glass half full" thoughts which have now become a natural part of my thought and life process. My new normal is happy, peaceful and grateful.

Another question

What is one small thing you can change that could make a big difference in your music career? Below are three changes I have made. Each has produced positive results in my music and on my music business bottom line.

* *Networking.* Actively building relationships at music conferences and online has directly led to multiple contract signings and thousands of additional annual dollars in income.

* *Learning from my peers.* I have developed a group of peers (from networking) who are much more skilled at various aspects of recording and business than I am. These people have freely shared their knowledge with me as have I with them. Their knowledge has quickly made my music better and resulted in an ability to get more placements and increase my net profits.

* *Scheduling.* A few years ago I became proactive in scheduling my daily and weekly songwriting and recording time. This change brought me a 200%-plus increase in my music production output. I used to produce about 50 tracks per year. Now my output is over 150 tracks annually. This change in scheduling has also resulted in my productions sounding better (the abundance principle) and has increased my annual revenue.

Results

The *small changes* I have made both in my life and in my music have led to BIG differences in what I now produce and receive. I am continually searching for my next "one small change" knowing that when I find and apply it good things will happen.

There is always something we have yet to discover. And sometimes those discoveries can have a huge impact upon our lives and livelihood.

Examine your life, music, and the way you conduct business. Look at the ways others successful in your field are doing their work. Are they doing something that could help you?

What is *one small thing* that could change your life in a big way today?

A New Perspective

I've got a quiz for you. No, it's not a written exam. No need to sweat.

Step 1

What I want you to do before you read any further is to look at this picture and tell me what you see.

Are you ready? Ok, go.

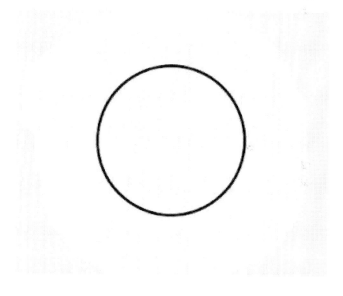

What do you see? Do you see a circle? The moon?

Do you see a round ball? Maybe you see the sun or the earth?

If you have a pen, pencil or iPad write down what you saw.

Step 2

Okay. Now let's go on to step two of the quiz.

Again, before you read any further, I want you to take a look at this next picture and tell me what you see. Here's a hint; it is a picture of the same thing you were looking at in the previous picture.

OK, go!

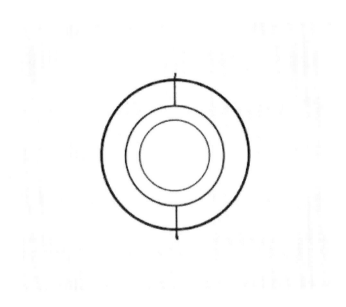

What do you see this time?

A flying saucer?

A pancake with lines in it?

Something else?

Again, write down what you saw.

Hang in there. We're almost done.

Step 3

Last part of the quiz. I am now going to give you a third picture of the same thing I showed you in the two previous pictures and I want you to tell me what you think it is.

Are you ready?

Go.

What is it?

A snowman?

Bingo!

You are correct.

Explain

Do you see it? All three pictures are of the exact same thing - a snowman. The first picture is looking at the snowman from the bottom up. The second picture is looking at the snowman from the top down. And the third picture is looking at the snowman head-on. Why didn't you see the snowman in picture one or picture two?

Perspective

It is amazing to me that in so many circumstances of life we can be looking at the exact same thing as someone else but because our *perspective* is different this very same thing looks quite dissimilar to each of us.

If we can step outside of our own feelings about politics or religion, for example, we will be able to see that often each political party or religion is looking to solve or explain the very same thing but they are stuck viewing those identical things from entirely different points of view.

This is not to say political parties and religions don't have very real differences. They most surely do. It is only to suggest that they also have some similarities which are quite often misconstrued as huge differences due to *perspective*.

Songs

It is a good practice when we are writing songs or composing music to try to get our mind around as many perspectives of our subject matter as we possibly can. Why? Communication. In all we do we are trying to communicate our ideas and stories to other people. One of our goals is to reach as many people as possible.

In order to most effectively communicate with others we need to understand *their* perspective. We need to see what *they* see and to know where *they* are coming from.

When we can see in multiple perspectives what happens? Our world view gets bigger and we are able to better identify, isolate and articulate those ideas universal to all perspectives. We can then *focus* on those universally seen concepts and more effectively communicate them to the largest amount of people.

We also can get closer to the Truth. And Truth is always a good thing. Deep down we all hunger for it.

Get curious about other people's perspective. Examine in. Mull it over. Run it through your own life experience. You will be more peaceful. You will gain a broader understanding, a greater acceptance and your music will communicate ever more powerfully with its listener.

Making Molehills out of Mountains

Let's face it. Most of us creative types struggle from time to time with emotions. It makes total sense. If we have the ability to create cool stuff with our thoughts it would follow that we also have the ability to create painful or negative stuff with our thinking.

Many people know that journalizing is a powerful tool in managing emotional and mental health challenges. The reason it is so powerful is that most depression and anxiety issues however big or small are magnified by (or even caused by) distorted thinking. It is a snowballing of negative thoughts.

Creative people can have a particularly difficult time with these mental challenges because it is their "job" to be *in their minds* much of the time. When negative thoughts run rampant in a person's mind, that person is easily susceptible to making themselves feel depressed and/or anxious.

Journalizing

The power of journalizing for mental health lies in two areas. First, it is simply empowering to be proactive in helping oneself. Actually *doing* something like this on a daily basis develops positive habits, confidence and promotes the internalization of good *stuff*.

Secondly, since the problem for many of those with depression and anxiety lies in distorted thinking a big part of the cure rests in clarity of thinking. Sorting out our thoughts.

Let me explain.

When we are bugged and feeling down or anxious it is because many, many thoughts are firing through our minds making our daily life problems seem overwhelmingly big and numerous. When we take ten or twenty minutes to write down what is actually on our minds, labeling those things bothering us, we will most often find it is usually only five or six things we need to deal with. Not the thousands of things we are telling ourselves.

And five or six daily life-challenges are easily manageable.

When we write down out thoughts (journalizing) and actually *see* that they are but a manageable few we will feel relief. We will become less anxious. We are less stressed and less down.

In addition to the relief we feel we will usually discover that half of our problems can be solved simply by letting go of *thinking of them* as problems. Sometimes in life there are real issues to deal with such as taking care of a sick child or getting new brakes for a car. But often the things we think are problems are things we can let go of if we put them in the proper light.

Additional benefits

I have been journalizing daily for nearly twenty years now. I started journalizing mainly to deal with my anxiety but have found there are many additional benefits to this practice.

I write in my journal for ten to twenty minutes each day. When I do this I am most often asking myself how I feel, what is on my mind, is anything bugging me and if so *why*. In doing this inventory many questions and answers emerge. Within those questions and answers I often find song titles and song stories. Bonus.

I never really journalize with the intent of looking for song titles and stories. My intent is simply to do some daily dusting off of the shelves in my *thinking*. Nevertheless titles and stories emerge.

Rules

There are no rules on how to journalize. No guidelines or parameters. No timeline you must adhere to. You can journalize for five minutes or fifty-five minutes every day.

There is only this one simple suggestion: be honest. Take an honest look at yourself and your thoughts and feelings and write them down.

Recap

So, why do I suggest journalizing? First and foremost for:

Clarity.

Keeping thoughts manageable.

Calming oneself down.

Making molehills out of mountains.

Secondly: For great song ideas.

These are the reasons I journalize daily. And my journalizing gives back to me all I am seeking and so much more.

Give it a try. You will be amazed by the gifts given to you.

Making a List – Checking it Twice

Has this ever been you?

"Today I think I'll work on redoing the drums for my library track due next week. Or maybe I'll cut an instrumental for that new show my publisher says is going into editing in a few days. No, there is a Justin Timberlake pitch possibility coming up. Maybe I should try to write something for that. Oh no! I just remembered I have two CDs due next month for another publisher. Maybe I should get started on them. But that band I've been working with wants me to send them a mix of the song we've been recording. Maybe I'll just get that done and sent off... Oh sheesh, I forgot about the Stax Trax CD I'm supposed to be finishing for my own company? Yikes! Forget it. I'll just have the last piece of apple pie in the fridge and watch some Ren and Stimpy on Netflix."

Overwhelmed

Do you ever feel overwhelmed? Do you ever have so much needing to be done that you can't seem to do one single thing?

One of the consequences of having a little success in music is that *a lot* of projects start rolling in. Projects from companies who wouldn't answer your email a year ago are now piling up on your desktop. I don't want to sound like I am whining here. Having work is a good thing. I have been without work before and I'll take the "drowning in work" option every time.

But sometimes I do get a bit overwhelmed with the deadlines and the ongoing opportunities I have. It can be difficult trying to weed through all of them trying to separate the great ones from the not-so-great ones. It can also be a bit of a challenge trying to decide whether to take a little *certain money* or to spend time on a project that *might* make you a bundle.

Often in the past I have just thrown up my hands paralyzed by too many options and retreated to the fridge for a snack and then to the TV for some mind-numbing vegetation time. My old escape plan - junk food and junk TV.

But all that usually left me with was the same old projects and decisions on my desktop and a stomach ache.

"There must be a better way," I would lament.

Organization

Let me tell you about this magical remedy I stumbled upon out of frantic necessity one morning. It wasn't even noon yet and I was feeling so overwhelmed with "to-do's" I had become yet again stalled and was standing with the refrigerator door wide open searching for a comforting piece of cheesecake.

"I can't be doing this to myself every day," I mumbled, "I need to stop now!"

With that I sat down at my kitchen counter with a piece of paper and a pen in hand and listed everything on my agenda. I started with the nearest deadlines and worked down in priority estimating the time it would take to do each chore and noting the hours alongside of every project. I broke it down into days of the week and left myself a couple of flex hours each day for unpredictables.

The list read something like this: (meals and breaks not included)

Monday:
    Cut track for Library "A": 10am - 2pm
    Run (jogging) 2:15 - 3:30
    Write pop or country pitches: 4pm - 9pm

Tuesday:
    Biz stuff and emails: 8:30am – 10am
    Cut track for Library A: 10am - 2pm
    Start writing/recording track for Library B: 2pm - 6pm
    Rehearse "live gig" band: 7pm - 9pm
    Work on lyrics for new stuff: 9pm - 11pm

Wednesday:
    Biz Stuff: 8am – 10am
    Cut track for Library A: 10am - 2pm
    Biz Meeting: 2:30pm - 4:00pm
    Run (jogging) 4:30pm - 5:45pm
    Upload 3 tracks to Library A: 6pm - 7pm
    Finish Library B track: 7pm - 9:pm

Thursday:
    Early meeting: 9am - 11am
    Record new pop song track: 11:30am - 4pm
    Run (jogging) 4:30pm - 6pm
    Finish pop song music: 7pm - 9:30pm
    Call/email and book vocalist: 9:30

Friday:
    Personal biz til noon
    Start new track for Library B: 12:30pm - 3:30pm
    Run (jogging) 3:30pm - 5pm
    Out to dinner with my wife

Saturday:
    Finish Library B track: 10am - 12noon
    Record vocalist on pop song: 1pm - 3pm
    Rough mix of pop song: 3pm - 4pm

Run (jogging)
Slam 2 easy tracks for Library A: 5pm - 11pm

Sunday:
Live gig day - no studio

Simple

I made a list. Simple, huh? I organized my work and my time. Every day that week I woke up with no stress and no feelings of being overwhelmed, just a clear picture of the tasks that needed to be accomplished throughout the week.

Did I veer from my plan? Of course I did. Stuff came up. Things need to be addressed immediately. But I had a list. I had a plan. I had some basic organization in my life which enabled me to be *much more productive* and *much less stressed*.

When I got the stuff *out of my mind* and *onto paper* (remember what I said before about journalizing?) it seemed entirely manageable. I made a molehill out of a perceived mountain. And I finished 8 songs. EIGHT songs! If I did that every week I would have over 400 new songs for the year. (Note that this particular week was pretty slammed with recording and writing. If I kept up that pace all year I would probably burn out fairly quickly.)

Moral of the story: If you are feeling overwhelmed and paralyzed - make a list.

As an old friend of mine used to say; "*Plan your work and work your plan.*"

Inspiration or Perspiration?

Inspiration or perspiration.

Which is it?

It's the age old question.

Is creativity (or the results of creativity) more inspiration or more perspiration?

I submit that it is both.

However, I would also submit that it is *a lot* more *perspiration* than inspiration.

Me

In my own personal day to day and week to week creative journey I have seen tiny, momentary flashes of inspiration lead to weeks of hard work trying to bring that inspiration to fruition.

I have also seen days upon days of hard work with no great ideas coming. But the hours are put in anyway. Those hours of labor plant the seeds, till the soil and water the ground until all at once an idea pushes through the dirt and a new artistic flower comes springing forth.

I love it when an idea comes to me out of the blue and I need to rush to get a pen and a piece of paper or sprint to find my hand held recorder hoping to capture the magic before it disappears.

I also greatly appreciate the toil and experimentation of a new project. The staring at a blank musical canvas with no idea whatsoever of what to paint. Those times where you try this and you try that but nothing seems to work - nothing seems to make sense.

Then suddenly amidst the labor comes a flash of light, a spark, an idea. You look at your work again and the dots start to connect, the music starts to flow like a roaring river and all you can do is hold on as you are swept away by melodies, rhythms and harmonies moving you ever further downstream toward some unknown destination.

Those moments are pure magic.

Others

In Daniel Cole's book *The Little Book of Talent* he cites numerous cases of talent hotbeds around the world where experts unanimously agree that talent is not *discovered* – it is *made*. It is developed from hard work, repetition, learning the craft, practice, dedication and attitude.

He finds again and again in his research the age old truth - *small actions repeated over time transform us*. This is the true reality of the most "talented" people. Like the way a professional golfer will spend hour after hour fine tuning his putt or the laboring tenacity of a guitar virtuoso running his scales up and down over and over until he can go no more. Daniel Cole discovers and documents the reality that there is absolutely no substitute for years of repetitive practice if one wishes to be highly successful in his or her chosen field.

It should not go unnoticed nor unexplored that the greatest talents in history are the ones who fail the most. Whether it is Michael Jordan (considered by many to be the greatest basketball player of all time) missing more shots than anyone else, or, as I've noted before, Thomas Edison who prior to inventing the light bulb discovered 1000 ways *not* to make a light bulb - the great ones frequently fail.

But they do not view their misses as failures. They simply view them as a necessary part of the process needed to get better.

Why are Michael Jordan, Billy Jean King, Thomas Edison or Michelangelo so extraordinarily successful? Because they put in the time.

Marathon

Great artistry is a marathon, not a sprint.

A good friend of mine talks in his music workshops about *growing quality out of quantity*. The idea is this: if you keep doing something again and again, whether it is writing songs and cues, learning an instrument, producing music, or whatever – even if at first you suck, over time you will *suck less*.

And given enough time, repetition and coaching you will move from "sucking less" into actual *quality*. And when you finally move into quality people will then proclaim you to have talent.

Progress

So is a successful creation more inspiration or perspiration? The answer is yes. It is both. But time-wise it is a lot more perspiration and a lot less inspiration. Probably well over 90% perspiration.

Don't be discouraged if you do not achieve perfection right away. The greatest talents, the experts in any field, are always looking less for *perfection* and more for *progress*. And progress will happen through practice, persistence and perspiration.

Take comfort in this: *If you have perspired, you will be inspired.*

Do the work and great things will come.

Takeaways (Chapters 53 – 61)

1. In the rewriting and editing process we need to keep in mind the potential marketability of our creations. (I.e. Can we change something to make our music more marketable while still maintaining its artistic integrity?)

2. Test your music out in public.

3. Don't rely solely on Grandma's opinion when discerning the marketability of your music.

4. Rejection is a big part of the music business.

5. Learn to "let rejection go" and move on.

6. If you can get a critique from those who reject your work – use it to learn and grow.

7. Remember to have fun while creating music. Your music will be better for it.

8. Positive changes in your lifestyle can have a positive effect on your career.

9. Try to examine the subject matter of your song lyrics from as many perspectives as possible. Your lyrics will have more depth and more universality.

10. Journaling can have great life benefits and can be the catalyst for some cool song ideas.

11. Keeping a daily and weekly work schedule will increase productivity and reduce stress.

12. A much greater amount of perspiration is needed (time-wise) than inspiration in the making of a successful music career.

Moods

By now you know that when writing cues for TV and other media we are most often called upon to write a particular mood, a combination of moods or a style conveying a certain mood. Here is a list of moods and styles to get your musical mind thinking in a new cue-like way.

Pick a few that work together. Then go write something.

Aggressive
Ambient
Angry
Anticipation
Anxious
Atmospheric
Ballad
Beautiful
Bluesy
Bold
Bouncy
Bright
Brooding
Calm
Campy
Carefree
Careful
Caring
Cartoon
Cautious
Celestial

Chaotic
Cheerful
Childlike
Confident
Confused
Cool
Dangerous
Dark
Delicate
Determined
Dirty
Distorted
Disturbing
Dramatic
Dreamy
Driving
Edgy
Eerie
Electronic
Elegant
Emotional
Energetic
Epic
Erotic
Ethereal
Ethnic
Evil
Exotic
Fear
Feel Good
Festive
Folksy
Fun
Funky
Funny
Futuristic
Gentle
Grungy
Happy
Haunting
Heartfelt
Heroic
Hopeful

Humorous
Hypnotic
Intense
Intrigue
Introspective
Jazzy
Joyful
Light
Majestic
Meditative
Melancholy
Mellow
Melodic
Moody
Mournful
Mysterious
Mystical
Oldies
Ominous
Patriotic
Peaceful
Pensive
Percussive
Playful
Positive
Powerful
Psychedelic
Pulsing
Quirky
Reflective
Relaxed
Rhythmic
Romantic
Sad
Scary
Sensual
Sentimental
Serene
Sexy
Silly
Sinister
Slapstick
Smooth

Soaring
Soft
Solemn
Soothing
Sophisticated
Soulful
Southern
Spacey
Sultry
Surreal
Suspenseful
Sweeping
Tender
Tense
Terror
Tribal
Triumphant
Uplifting
Urgent
Vengeful
Vibrant
Warm
Weepy
Whimsical
Wistful
Yearning
Zany

Resources

People often ask me, "How do I get started in the film and TV music business?" There are many different roads and avenues one can take to begin their journey. The most important thing is not *where* you start but *that* you start.

Certainly doing research on the internet is a valuable tool today that didn't exist just a few short years ago. Looking up contact information for music supervisors, music libraries and publishing companies is a snap in this day and age. Just remember when contacting any business to be professional and respectful.

I always recommend that people consider joining an organization called Taxi (taxi.com). They are highly reputable and I have personally secured many deals through them. There is a small fee to join and a nominal submission fee to submit music to their screeners. Upon joining you will receive new listings every two weeks from companies looking for specific types of music. You then may choose to submit your music for consideration to these listings or not. Once a member, you will also get free admission to one of the best music conferences on the planet (put on by Taxi) each November in the Los Angeles area.

Performing rights organizations are also a good place to start. ASACP, BMI, SESAC, SOCAN and the rest all have helpful personnel who are there to guide you and answer your questions. In addition, they all have numerous conferences and workshops where you can learn and network. All of their contact information can be found on the internet.

Of course, traveling to one of the major music cities (or moving there) and pounding the pavement is another path toward making headway in the biz. I have done this extensively in Nashville with positive results. In the USA, Nashville, New York and LA are home to many of the companies you most likely will want to work with.

It is always a good thing to meet face to face with potential business partners.

Don't discount the emerging markets. My own Seattle backyard is home to companies such as Microsoft and Amazon (as well as over 150 gaming companies) who may well become the next generation's ABC, NBC, and CBS.

Remember, the internet is your friend. Searching through production music sites, music libraries, songwriting forums and the like will give you a wealth of information you can use to cross reference and find the most suitable path to pursue. Research, research, research.

Conclusion

It is my great hope that within these pages you have found some informative "nuggets" – some tips and tricks you can put to use right away in your musical journey. I hope too that a few "a-ha" moments have flickered on inside your mind and that you have maybe found a missing puzzle piece or two somewhere in my stories.

I want to encourage you to keep pursuing your passion and dreams. Don't be discouraged. Great things will happen for you with patience, perseverance and practice.

Remember the old saying, *Rome wasn't built in a day*? There may be times when it feels like the construction of your city will never be finished but don't lose faith. You will build your Rome if you just keep taking it one step at a time.

In conclusion I will wish for you one more cliché: *Stop and smell the roses*. Take a look around. Enjoy the moments. This is your life. These days are *your* story. You get to write it. Make it a great one. Revel in the people you meet. Marvel at all of the amazing colors that make up the character of the human race. Embrace life's music and dare to dance with it.

And one more thing: Above all, *love one another*. Share with and help other people. If you do this it will come back to you tenfold and your life will be an astonishing success of the very best kind.

Acknowledgments

They say it takes a village to raise a child. I think it may have taken an entire city to grow this musician's career. Thank you Mom and Dad for making me take guitar lessons when all I wanted to be was a Beatle. Thanks especially to my wife Karin for marrying this crazy musician and for always supporting my goofy dreams. Thanks to my daughters Crystal, Tessa and Kelsey – you are the true music of my life.

I want to give a big shout out to Michael Laskow and my family at Taxi (Taxi.com) for teaching me what a "cue" is and to always *pay it forward.* You guys rock! There are so many songwriting, musician and producer friends who have taught me along the way and keep teaching me. I don't want to forget anyone so I will just lump you all into one great big giant group hug and say a heartfelt Thank You!

I want to call out a few people who were there at the beginning of my studio and songwriting career slugging it out with me and who continue to inspire: Bruce Johnson, Erik Hall, Chip Wilson and Scott Krippayne – so much respect and appreciation.

Thank you Kelsey Krippaehne for your eagle eye in editing this book and Tessa Krippaehne for helping me to get it published. RMC Publishing – yeah, baby!

Also, a heartfelt thanks to Dr. David Penner and my spiritual teachers for helping me find my marbles. It's hard to do anything when you've lost your marbles.

Lastly, I want to thank the unseen Power that has created all that is. Life is beautiful. May I spend the rest of my days giving back.

Glossary

ASCAP: The *American Society of Composers, Authors and Publishers* is a performing rights organization.

BMI: *Broadcast Music, Inc.* is a performing rights organization.

BPM: Beats per minute.

Cue: A recorded piece of music used in Film and TV.

DAW: Digital audio workstation.

DI: Direct Input or Direct Box.

EQ: Equalization or equalizer - a tone control system that allows you to boost or cut certain frequencies in an audio system.

FX: Effects such as reverb, delay and compression.

Track: A track can be a song or a musical cue. It also can be one recorded element of a song (I.e. The bass track).

Mic: Microphone

Mixing (or the mix): Most often refers to the placement or "mixing" of all of the instruments and sounds in a song.

Music Library: A company with thousands of recorded music cues in various genres available for licensing.

Music Supervisor: The person whose job it is to find the right music for a TV show or Film.

Overdubbing: The process recording additional sounds (instruments or vocals) on an existing recording.

Panning: The spread of the sound signal (instruments) anywhere between hard left (8 o'clock) and hard right (4 o'clock) in a stereo mix.

Placement: (Getting a placement) Getting one of your cues or songs used in a TV show, film or other media.

PRO: A performing rights organization a la ASCAP, BMI, SESAC. SOCAN.

Quantize: A digital process of transforming imperfectly performed (MIDI) rhythmic notes into mathematically precise notes.

Sample: A sample is a recorded sound or tone used to create a virtual instrument.

SESAC: Originally the *Society of European Stage Authors and Composers*, is the smallest of the three performance rights organizations in the US.

SOCAN: The Society of Composers, Authors and Music Publishers of Canada is a performing rights organization.

Spreadsheets: Every cue will have a basic spreadsheet of information. The elements vary but often include: Title, bpm, song key, moods, description, lead instruments, writer info, publishing info and PRO info.

TAXI: (Taxi.com) is an independent A&R company.

Virtual Instrument: A musical instrument or sound that is triggered using software in a computer environment.

Bibliography

Drive, Daniel H. Pink, © 2009 by Daniel H. Pink, Published by the Penguin Group, New York, NY.

Little Bets, Peter Sims, © 2011 by Peter Sims, Free Press, A Division of Simon & Schuster, Inc. New York, NY.

FutureHit.DNA, Jay Frank, © 2009 by Jay Frank, Published by Futurehit, Inc. Nashville Tennessee.

Hack Your Hit, Jay Frank, © 2012 by Jay Frank, Published by Futurehit, Inc. Nashville Tennessee.

Here, There and Everywhere, Geoff Emerick and Howard Massey, © 2006 by Emerick Softpaw Productions, Inc. and Howard Massy, Gotham Books, Penguin Group (USA) Inc. New York, NY.

Making Rumours, Ken Caillat with Steven Stiefel, © 2012 by Ken Caillat and Steven Stiefel, Published by John Wiley and Sons, Inc. Hoboken, New Jersey.

Recording Magazine Editors' Blog, Lorenz Rychner, © June 11, 2012, www.recordingmag.com/blogs.html.

Fetts Mixing Roadmap, Fett, © 2013 by Fett, Azalea Music Publications, Nashville, TN.

So Good They Can't Ignore You, Cal Newport, © 2012 by Calvin C. Newport, Business Plus, Hachette Book Group, New York, NY.

On Writing, Stephen King, © 2000 by Stephen King, Scribner - A division of Simon & Schuster, Inc. New York, NY.

The Little Book of Talent, Daniel Coyle, © 2012 by Daniel Coyle, Published in the United States by Bantam Books, Random House, Inc. New York.

Small is the New Big, Seth Godin, © Do You Zoom, Inc. 2006, published by the Penguin Group, New York, NY.

Tribes, Seth Godin, © Do You Zoom, Inc. 2008, Published by the Penguin Group, New York, NY.

What Technology Wants, Kevin Kelly, © Kevin Kelly 2010, Published by the Penguin Group, New York, NY.

The Musician's Guide to Licensing Music, Darren Wilsey, with Daylle Deanna Schwartz, © 2010 by Darren Wilsey and Daylle Deanna Schwartz, Billboard Books, Crown Publishing Group, New York.

Making Music, Edited by George Martin, © Shuckburgh Reynolds Ltd with the exception of pages 74 to 77 © Stephen Sondhiem, William Morrow and Company, Inc. New York, NY.

Nuendo Power, Ashley Shepherd and Robert Guerin, © 2004 by Thomson Course Technology PTR, Boston MA.

The Musician's Guide to Home Recording, Peter McIan and Larry Wichman, © 1988 by Peter McIan and Larry Wichman, Linden Press/Fireside, New York, NY.

Home Recording Boot Camp, Ronan Chris Murphy, 2007, workshop at Taxi Road Rally Conference, Los Angeles, CA. (Taxi.com).

Hit Song Boot camp, Robin Frederick, 2007, workshop at Taxi Road Rally Conference, Los Angeles, CA. (Taxi.com).

The Difference Between a Song and a Hit Song, Ralph Murphy, 2011, Seminar at Taxi Road Rally Conference, Los Angeles, CA. (Taxi.com).

Production Music Association (PMA), "What's the Value of Music, 2012?," Panel Discussion - Nashville, TN.

Digital Music News, (digitalmusicnews.com), © 2012

1000 conversations and workshops with fellow Composer Camp music creators.

Dean Krippaehne

ABOUT THE AUTHOR

Dean Krippaehne is a veteran songwriter, musician and Film & TV music producer. His many credits include: *Duck Dynasty, The Oprah Winfrey Show, Smash, One Life to Live, Parenthood, The Vampire Diaries, The Dr. Oz Show, The Today Show, Say Yes to the Dress, CBS This Morning, Biography A&E, Super Soul Sunday, The Hills, Switched At Birth, Oprah's Oscar Special, Haunted Collector, Best Ink, T-Mobile and dozens more.* As a songwriter he has earned two gold and platinum records and a Billboard Top 10. Dean also co-founded the jingle company *Spektrum Productions* and in 1987 opened up Seattle's *Tri-West Recording Studios*. In 2011 he founded All Screen Music (allscreenmusic.com) and currently lives happily with his wife, dog and cat in Seattle.

Made in the USA
Middletown, DE
08 July 2017